Critical Praise for *Finding the Groove*

"Music educators are hardly the only people who can benefit from the considerable wisdom contained within *Finding the Groove*, Jeremy Steinkoler's book about the lessons he's gleaned from his years as a drummer and drum teacher. A pithy storyteller who makes his points in sharp, clean strokes, he's as canny and perceptive about human nature and the intricate pulse of student/mentor interactions as he is about trap set fundamentals. Drawing on gigs he's played and encounters with musical colleagues obscure and legendary, Steinkoler shows how he's applied hard-won knowledge to his countless lessons with students both motivated and slacking. Ultimately, *Finding the Groove* offers profound lessons for teaching or pursuing just about any creative endeavor."

—*Andrew Gilbert (San Francisco Chronicle)*

"While *Finding the Groove* is ostensibly about drummers and drumming, what Jeremy Steinkoler is really offering in this eminently readable and perceptive collection of essays is some keen insight into the human condition, specifically as it relates to the 'big questions' that inevitably confront musicians as we move through life plying our craft. Each essay presents economical, articulate, usable nuggets of wisdom, gleaned from a life's work as drummer, educator, and seeker of knowledge. My teacher Freddie Gruber used to ask the Zen Koan-like question, 'How can you know the difference, if you don't know the difference?' *Finding the Groove* is certainly a first step in the right direction for any musician looking to understand what that 'difference' is all about."

—*Daniel Glass (Royal Crown Revue, Brian Setzer)*

"Throughout every page, Jeremy makes abundantly clear his dedication and ability to expand the music-minds of current and future drummers. If you want to learn to think more deeply about your art and to be emboldened in a way that triggers your spark, *Finding the Groove* is an absolute must-read!"

—*Nate Brown (Founder/Publisher, onlinedrummer.com)*

"Jeremy's book is laid out like a song form, which is a very important bit of knowledge in itself. When I was coming up, learning how to play songs was a big part of learning to play the drums. As you read, you'll see what he has learned through his musical experiences— life lessons! My favorite teachers always me taught that drumming is more than paradiddles. The title says it all. Enjoy!"

—*David Garibaldi (Tower of Power)*

"Steinkoler brings a sense of empathy and wonder that adds weight to the lessons at hand. Drum instructors in particular will find lots to chew on, but the rest of us will recognize much of ourselves here as well—who we are, who we were, and who we hope to become."

—*Moderndrummer.com*

"Jeremy Steinkoler's *Finding the Groove* is full of life lessons, musings, and stories from the life of a drummer, delivered by a man who is clearly passionate about his craft. From the responsibilities and challenges of the teacher, to the mental aspects that create confidence, *Finding the Groove* is a fun yet thought-provoking read that will inspire, educate, and entertain you, especially if you share a passion for drumming and teaching."

—*Joe Bergamini (Drummer, Author, Hudson Music Editor, Sabian Education Network Director)*

"One of my favorite ever reads! You can tell that everything within the pages of Jeremy's book is the result of decades of passion and experience. Reading it can only lead to a greater understanding of the universal language that we all love—music! Whether you're a drummer, artist, composer, or teacher, this is a must-read!"

—*Tony McNally (Drummer/Educator, Founder of ToneAlly)*

"I've read Jeremy's book for a third time, and I plan on reading it again. *Finding the Groove* is a book that is just packed full of experience, strength, and hope for the drumming community at large. I've discovered things in this book that have truly inspired me. I highly recommend it to drummers of all ages! Great book!"

—*Chip Ritter (Drummer/Educator,
Co-founder Drummers Education Connection)*

"Well written, clear, interesting, and practical—a real contribution to the world of drumming."

—*Joel Rothman (World's most prolific drum book author)*

"Jeremy's book is an amazing amalgamation of drum wisdom, humor, anecdotes, philosophy, and the inner game of drumming. It's a practical guide to understanding the core necessities needed to become a professional musician."

—*Chris Brady (Aquarian Drumheads)*

"Jeremy's book *Finding the Groove* instantly hit me like he was writing about my own teaching and music performing experiences! It reawakened so many memories about my journey of becoming a private music teacher, which includes all the different hats we must wear to succeed. This is an absolute must-read for all drummers, drum teachers, and passers of the musical torch of music and life!"

—*Jim Royle (Drummer/Educator,
Owner/Director Jim Royle Drum Studio)*

"*Finding the Groove* is the ultimate resource for musicians seeking insight, inspiration, and knowledge about the world of drumming. With his decades of experience as a drum teacher and performer, Jeremy helps you to understand how to develop drumming talent— and apply it in the real world! It's so full of valuable information that I feel it is an essential read for all drummers, and especially my students. I couldn't read it fast enough! *Finding the Groove* inspires me and my students to be excited about drumming and to better ourselves in every way possible. I highly recommend this book!"

—*Rick Stojak (Drummer/Educator, Co-founder Drummers Education Connection)*

"*Finding the Groove* should be in the hands of every aspiring drummer—even every aspiring musician—because it contains decades of wisdom in its pages. I wish I had a book like this when I started out playing. Teachers, I would make this required reading for all of your students!"

—*Jean Fineberg (David Bowie, Sister Sledge, Joe Cocker)*

"*Finding the Groove* is equal parts practical and philosophical, like a *Letters to a Young Poet* for the modern drummer. It's clearly designed to be the best friend of any aspiring drummer, but its lessons were potent to me even as a pianist and songwriter. I especially appreciated the personal anecdotes, which helped to demystify some of the more daunting aspects of making one's way in the field of music. I've had the pleasure of playing with Jeremy on a few occasions, and it was fun to see that he writes as he plays... thoughtfully, incisively, and with great care."

—*Rachel Efron (Singer/Songwriter)*

"Jeremy's powerful book, *Finding the Groove*, transported me back in time to the magic I felt purchasing my first drum set. It's a book that reminds us of important lessons we've learned and wisdom we hope to gain—both in music and in life. This book isn't just for drummers. It's relatable for any musician or anyone who pursues a passion. I highly recommend it!"

—*Kelli Rae Tubbs (Drummer/Historian)*

"*Finding the Groove* is reminiscent of the writings of the great Roy Burns. Within the pages of this book one is reminded that as musicians, and more importantly as music educators, we need to hold ourselves to the standard of being the best we can be on a daily basis, as we are called upon to pass on the traditions of greatness that came before us. Discover your greatness in *Finding the Groove*."

—*Bart Robley (Drummer/Educator,*
Co-founder Drummers Education Connection)

"I found Jeremy's book to be both entertaining and insightful—a pleasure to read. As a drummer and teacher, it contains many relatable and familiar stories, along with unique insights. But this isn't just a book for drummers—people from all walks of life will be able to relate to so many aspects of his experience."

—*Dawn Richardson (4 Non Blondes, Tracy Chapman)*

"Being a successful working musician requires talent, vision, discipline, social skills, and some sort of business sense. Each one of these qualities requires study, insight, guidance, and support. Jeremy's passion and longtime experience as a talented teacher, and equally talented professional drummer, provide all the above in this wonderful read."

—*John Mader (John Fogerty, Bonnie Raitt, Hamilton)*

FINDING *the* GROOVE

LESSONS FROM A LIFE IN
DRUMMING, TEACHING, AND PERFORMING

JEREMY STEINKOLER

Finding the Groove
by Jeremy Steinkoler

Digital version published by Hudson Music
www.hudsonmusic.com

Book design by Michele Friedman

CONTENTS

BRIDGE: *Drumming in the World*

SOLO: *For Musicians of All Stripes*

CODA: *Life Lessons*

INTRODUCTION

The idea for this book came to me slowly, over the course of a couple of years. Every so often, I'd feel the urge to write about a lesson I taught or an experience I had, some bit of wisdom I thought worth sharing. But I wasn't in the habit of writing much since my days studying literature in college. I'd published a couple of articles on drumming, but for the most part, I would just share these stories with some of my students during their lessons.

The longer I've been playing drums and teaching, the more I wanted to get down on paper a record of what I feel are some of the more important things I've learned—bits of wisdom that I felt would be of use to other drummers and musicians, lessons I wish I had learned when I was a young drummer.

I found that as I started to write, many of the stories and lessons tumbled forward onto the page, as if they were piled up in a closet ready to burst open with the slightest turn of the doorknob. I furiously scribbled down sketches and scraps, concepts I wanted to communicate and experiences I wanted to share that I felt were important or meaningful, or in some way had an impact on me.

Other stories had to be teased out, anecdotes or experiences I had forgotten until I shined a light on the dusty shelves of my past, some of which, I realized upon reflection, had shaped the musician, teacher, and person that I am today.

The essays herein are the distillations of many, many hours of drumming, teaching drum lessons and band workshops, performing, practicing, parenting, and living: a compendium of what I've learned so far. The more I've learned, the more I've realized how little I actually know. I believe we must always question, think critically, and strive to take our understanding to a deeper level.

I believe that many of the lessons contained herein apply not just to drummers and musicians. Some of them, I hope, will resonate with anyone who pursues a passion or hones a practice. I invite readers to pick and choose the essays that might interest them. There is no need to read the book in any particular order. In fact, I think the last several essays might resonate with more people than the content more specific to drumming and drummers. In any case, even if not all of the stories resonate with everyone, I hope some of them will at least make readers question and think and lead them to their own truths.

In several essays I refer to BandWorks, which is a rock 'n' roll band workshop program that I started with my guitarist friend Steve Gibson in 1993. BandWorks began as an idea for us to get some of our students together to play music, since at the time (before the Internet), it was more challenging for musicians to find others to play with. But as the program evolved and grew, we realized that we weren't just connecting musicians with one another to share in the experience of playing in a band—we were also teaching the values of listening, cooperation, and collaboration toward a common goal.

Since then, BandWorks has grown into a robust program with rock band workshops, clinics, and summer camps at locations around the San Francisco Bay Area. We've served thousands of musicians over the years, and we are proud to have created a thriving, inclusive, and supportive community of musicians.

I could not possibly have written this book without so many influences that have shaped my understanding of drumming and teaching: from hundreds of hours taking my own lessons, to thousands of hours of teaching lessons, to my instructors who have tutored me in other disciplines (notably golf, archery, and baseball), and to my life instructors—my son Evan, my stepson Griffin, my students, my friends, and most importantly, my wife Michele. I remain a student of the drums after 40 years of playing, and am always learning new things about teaching after 30 years of giving lessons. On we go...

INTRO

My Story/Lessons from Teaching

MY FIRST DRUM SET

"But I *need* a drum set!" I pleaded. "They're not *that* loud, and I promise I'll keep the door closed!"

I was 10 years old. For several months before I started taking drum lessons, I would bombard my parents with constant pleas for a drum kit. I'm not sure I even knew what it meant, to play the drums. I was certain that *having* a drum set would be cool, and would immediately make me cooler, at least in my own mind, if not those of my friends. But I had no real notion of what *playing* the drums was about. All I knew was that I was tired of my piano lessons, and that playing the drums couldn't be nearly as boring as practicing my scales and god-awful easy piano pieces.

After taking weekly lessons and practicing on a pad (a measly practice pad!) for six months, my desire to play on a real drum set had reached epic proportions. Seeing that my interest had not abated, my parents finally relented. So one fateful evening after school, we took a taxi to West 48th St. in New York City, a magical boulevard lined with more than a dozen music stores. I counted down the blocks as we slowly made our way across town, drumming on my legs the entire ride. When we finally arrived, I burst out of the taxicab before my father had even paid the driver, jumping onto the sidewalk and pressing my face against the window of the nearest music store, ogling the shiny new drum kits stacked up like towers of giant, rare jewels. "How about that one? I asked, "Or that one?" "Oooh, look at that one! That one totally rocks!" I exclaimed. My dad put his hand on my shoulder and smiled.

With the help of my drum teacher who met us at the store, we settled on a red wine-colored Rogers 5-piece kit and a set of Paiste cymbals, which I still own. We managed to cram them all into a taxicab for the ride home, drums bouncing on our laps as we drove over bumps and potholes. I beamed with pride as I helped tote them up to our apartment on the 5th floor. I was a real drummer!

Of course I barely knew how to play. But I had a drum kit, and I could play a few beats, and for some unknown but fortuitous alignment of the stars, our neighbors in our apartment building never complained. The rock and roll world didn't know what was coming, of that I was sure....

I try to remember what that was like for me as a 10-year old when I go help my students purchase their first set of drums. I've done it so many times it's practically just a routine. But I never get tired of watching my young students' faces when they walk into the drum shop, beaming with excitement and anticipation just as mine did 40 years ago. They pay no attention as I explain to their parents about the resonant qualities of maple vs. mahogany, the tonal differences between single and double-ply drumheads, or the benefits and drawbacks of double-braced hardware. I can feel their excitement. And I share it too—not the excitement of a new drum set, but the excitement of possibility, of helping to launch a new drummer into the world, to push him or her on a journey of musical and self-exploration, connecting with other human beings in this unique creative endeavor...and because sometimes the journey to the Rock and Roll Hall of Fame starts with the purchase of a new drum kit.

THE ALLURE OF THE DRUM

When I meet with a beginning student for the first time, I will always start the lesson by asking why they are interested in playing the drums. Typically, people will say, "I just think they're cool," or, "I've always wanted to learn to play," or something to that effect. There's just something about the drums that speaks to people. It also helps that there is no complex array of buttons or valves or strings, no immediate barriers between you and making a sound. Just a stick of wood in each hand, and that's it.

People are drawn to the drums for different reasons. I think there is something very primal to them, some innate, instinctive, almost *animal* appeal (remember the Muppet who played the drums?). After all, as soon as we're born, *we are rhythm.* Our hearts beat in time according to a regular pulse—and it swings! There is rhythm everywhere in nature: in the orbits of the planets and stars, the cycles of light and dark, the changing of the seasons, in migration cycles, and in movement. There is rhythm in just about everything we humans do: walk, sleep, eat, breathe...and we run into trouble when these rhythms are disrupted.

The universe, after all, began with a Big Bang: *the first downbeat,* from which all time and existence came forth. Ever since, rhythm has been a part of the natural world. So it makes sense that on some level we are all drummers, drawn to the drums, with which we can create our own rhythms and tap into this unique dimension of our existence that binds the universe together.

When I was a junior in college, I led a weekly drum circle for several months. Everyone was welcome, and there was no requirement to know how to play any percussion instruments in order to participate. Each "jam" would last somewhere between 5–20 minutes. Sometimes we'd try to shape the arc of each session with dynamics, but for the most part, it would just evolve organically. Those who were beginners would just tap along simple patterns in time, while the more experienced players would layer more complex rhythms over the basic pulse. We'd take turns "soloing," or highlighting each individual's improvisations, going around the room focusing on one person at a time. There was no spiritual component to the drum circle, at least not formally. We'd talk about listening and locking into the beat together, and there was an implication that some higher connection was possible through the experience of drumming *together in time.*

For many years, if I ever mentioned my experiences with the drum circle to my friends, I'd joke dismissively that it was during my short-lived "hippie" phase. But as I think about the intrinsic allure of the drums that speaks to so many people, I find myself reconsidering how I frame those experiences. Even though it was rough-hewn and rudimentary from a musical standpoint, there was something about that experience of tapping into the beat together that *was* spiritual. Somehow, through this strange medium—one night a week for 90 minutes—we found community and compassion, and we always left feeling better than when we arrived.

HOW I GOT STARTED TEACHING DRUMS

One summer day in 1991, I was hanging out with my friend Jamie Rusling at Herb David's Guitar shop in Ann Arbor, Michigan, where he worked as a salesperson. I had recently started working at nearby Oz's Music, a shop my friend Steve Osburn, a local classical guitarist and Chapman Stick player, had opened. Jamie was a mutual friend of mine and Steve's—the music scene in Ann Arbor wasn't all that large, and even as a college student, I knew a lot of the local cats, many of whom I'd become acquainted with while working at Oz's.

Jamie was an accomplished and inspired percussionist. I'd met him through the weekly drum circle he'd started, and we quickly became good friends. We played a lot of music together while I attended college, and with his support and encouragement, he helped me on my path. He also introduced me to the doumbek, an hourglass-shaped Middle Eastern ceramic drum that became one of my side pursuits when I wasn't playing the drum kit.

When we weren't busy, Jamie and I would occasionally drop by the stores to shoot the breeze. One afternoon, as we were hanging out invariably talking about drums, a young college student walked into the shop and inquired about getting some lessons. "Well, I don't teach traps, but my friend Jeremy here does, and I'm sure he'll charge you the same low rate that I do," Jamie said, smiling at me. Flustered, I introduced myself to the student and took down his number. When he left, I turned to Jamie. "What are you talking about man, you know I don't teach drum lessons!?" "You'll be great at it," he assured me. "You're a great communicator, and it'll give you a chance to get back to basics and make some extra money at the same time." I looked at him skeptically. "Trust me," he said.

I trusted him. I gave the student a call, and let him know that I'd never taught before. "That's OK," he replied. "I've never taken lessons before." "Well," I said, "I can show you what I know and what's worked for me. But I don't really know what I'm doing as far as teaching goes." It turned out he lived just a couple of blocks from me, so I started going over to his place once a week for lessons. I think I charged him ten dollars an hour.

Jamie was right. I did enjoy it. It was fun to get back to the fundamentals, to help people learn how to play and hear them improve. I ended up picking up a few more students and was able to make some decent money teaching in my freezing cold garage, where, despite the space heater, my students and I could see our breath in the frigid Michigan winter air. At the music store, I checked out new drumming books I'd never heard of, and I started organizing some teaching materials of my own. I think I had four or five students until I graduated and left for California, where winter doesn't really exist.

I often think back to that day at the music shop. It's funny to look back at your life and see how impactful certain events were, when at the time they did not seem all that significant. I try to keep that in mind in my teaching practice and trust that some of the work that I do—that all teachers do—will have a meaningful impact on people's lives, often in ways that won't be clear for years to come.

WE ARE ALWAYS LEARNING

I started taking lessons with Norman Grossman when I was in high school. I studied with him for four years. He was an accomplished freelance jazz player, had written two instructional books, and toured with some famous big bands. I respected him immensely. At the first lesson, I asked him how long he'd been playing. "Over 40 years," he replied. My eyes just about popped out of my head. "Wow, you must be really good!" I said. "Well," he replied, "You don't keep getting that much better after the first 15 years or so."

At the time, not knowing any better, I took him at his word. And maybe that's how it went for him. For several years I operated under this assumption, based on that one conversation at our first meeting. And though he was a great teacher and I owe him so much, he was dead wrong about this one thing: you're never done getting better.

Even if you don't spend the same number of hours practicing every day, there are many other ways to learn and improve. I learn something every time I go out to hear a show. It might be some particular groove or fill that I jot down in my little notebook, or it could be about stage presence or attitude. I learn every day from my students, who frequently come up with creative ways of interpreting some exercise or applying some concept that I hadn't thought of. Naturally, I learn from listening to music, watching videos, and talking to other musicians and teachers. I also glean a lot from transcribing (writing out drum parts, melodies, or passages from recordings). And of course, I improve from practicing and from playing with other musicians. While some of these methods of learning may not be the same as woodshedding rudiments, they all have a positive impact on my playing and help me grow as a player.

Consider also that music is not static, but dynamic by nature. Evolution, after all, is the driving force behind art and creativity. What if, as a jazz saxophonist in the 1940s, you ignored the innovation of Charlie Parker? Or, as an R&B drummer in the mid-1960s, you didn't pay attention to what Jabo Starks and Clyde Stubblefield were doing in James Brown's band? Trends and new creative paradigms would pass you by, and you'd miss out on new avenues of musical potential. You'd limit your creative horizon. Artists are constantly traversing new territory, paving the way for those who come after them. You have to pay attention, or you'll get stuck where you are without any kind of map to navigate the future.

I remember seeing the great jazz drummer Al Foster play with tenor saxophonist Joe Henderson, and watching him hit two drums at the same time with one stick, holding it sideways in the middle like a baton. *You can't do that!* I remember thinking, as if I could tell Al Foster what he could do. I once heard Elvin Jones, the brilliant and innovative drummer with John Coltrane, swing so hard while whaling on the snare drum on the two and four, which went against everything I knew about playing jazz. I listened to Jason McGerr of Death Cab for Cutie talk about using his left foot to play 16th notes on the hi-hat in-between the 8th notes of his right hand, which at the time was a totally new concept to me. And I watched, dumbfounded, as the drummer Trilok Gurtu played his drums sitting down on the floor like they were some giant set of tabla. I have countless recollections of people like these bucking trends, breaking conventions, being creative. As soon as you think you know the only way to do something, someone comes along and shows you a different way to do it.

In addition to learning unfamiliar things, we can also learn by digging deeper into things we already know, revealing layers of subtlety and complexity that were not apparent on the surface.

One of the books I use in my teaching practice is *Future Sounds* by David Garibaldi, the drummer from the seminal funk band Tower of Power. It's a great book, full of inventive permutations of mostly linear funk grooves, where only a single limb strikes a surface at one time, as opposed to playing simultaneously, as is common in most other styles. He moves the entire groove over one 16th note per exercise, so that each time you play it, you're starting in a different spot. He does it 16 times, so that you end up with the same coordination pattern phrased 16 different ways. It's incredible how different the grooves sound and feel, and it reveals how stuck we've been in framing funk grooves in the same way for so long.

I had a student who was fortunate enough to take a couple of lessons with David. It turned out that several years after he had written it, David was still practicing exercises out of his own book. Similarly, when the noted jazz pianist Hank Jones died, they found a book of exercises open on his piano that he had been practicing out of. It was a book he had written.

THE BEST TEACHERS AREN'T JUST TEACHERS

The best teachers aren't just teachers, and the best coaches aren't just coaches—they're *role models* and *mentors*.

As the father of a 15-year old and a 26-year old stepson, I can say unequivocally that parenting is one of the most challenging endeavors there is. You're responsible not only for your child's physical health and well-being, but also for their emotional health; for helping them learn to respect themselves and those around them, and to be able to engage in healthy relationships and be good citizens of the world. A tall order, especially when it's challenging enough to do it yourself!

As parents, we need allies. It's an enormous responsibility to raise a healthy kid, so why not recruit as much help as possible? It could be a family friend, a coach, a tutor, a schoolteacher, or a music teacher. Sometimes, when it's a good fit, these relationships can be truly transformative. They can help kids and teens navigate their paths to adulthood and have a profound impact on who they become later in life.

I'm a big believer in finding the right fit with your private music teacher. This goes way beyond reputation and curriculum (though content is important, naturally; I wouldn't want my son working with a piano teacher who wasn't teaching him to read music, for example, or with a teacher who wasn't working with him on improvising by ear). It's critical to me that my son's teacher is organized, patient, is a very good communicator, is a strong player in addition to being a good teacher, runs more or less on time (*time* is a life skill, not just a musical one, after all), and most importantly, is dedicated to their teaching practice.

If I'm paying someone to teach my kid to play music or sports, they need to be committed to teaching and helping people learn, and not just doing it to make some extra cash on the side while they subsidize their professional career. Kids aren't stupid. They know right away if a teacher is their advocate and has their best interest in mind, or is mailing it in to pay the bills.

I want my son to look up to his teacher, for him or her to be a role model. I want his teacher to model responsibility to one's self and to one's musical practice; to celebrate musical successes and support musical failures; and, ultimately, to help my son find his own musical voice, and not try to turn him into some clone of their style of playing or paint-by-numbers product of their pedagogical method.

As a student—and I will always consider myself a student—I've taken lessons with a number of different teachers with very different approaches. And since I've been a professional, I've taken a handful of lessons with some of the great players alive today. But I've found that the teachers I've learned the most from have typically been those who had a dedicated teaching practice, and who were used to communicating and formulating coherent ideas about their playing and their conceptual approach. And these have not necessarily been the best players, nor the most famous.

TEACH YOUR CHILDREN WELL

When I was 16, I wanted nothing more than to please my drum teacher (aside from wanting to make out with Lisa Fishman). I had been taking weekly lessons with him for a couple of years, and my skills had improved dramatically under his tutelage. I looked forward to my lesson each week, and I was always excited to find out what new concept he was going to teach me, which new puzzle I would have to solve.

When I'd arrived at high school a couple of years earlier, I'd already been playing drums for a few years, but I had never been very disciplined with my practicing. In fact, from about the age of 12 to 14, my drums had mostly collected dust in the corner of my room. Inspired by my new teacher and new opportunities to play, I spent the summer of my sophomore year practicing my tail off, and I got pretty good fairly quickly (at least good enough to play in my high school jazz band and combo, and to impress Lisa Fishman).

I've been teaching drums now for the past 30 years and playing professionally since I graduated from college. Tens of thousands of sticking exercises, several albums, and many hundreds of gigs later, I've learned a lot about drumming, and a lot about music. But I think I've learned more about the importance of relationships.

When you embark on a career in music, you tend not to think much about relationships. Your head is filled with artistic vision, hope, ambition, and some balance of humility and pride, confidence and trepidation. Along the way, it's easy to forget that we all start out the same, as beginners.

My son is 15 now, and is an accomplished jazz pianist. A few years ago we found him a piano teacher, a young, eager, local jazz musician whom I hadn't played with, but who was recommended by a friend. The truth is, as a professional musician, you're never more than one degree of separation from pretty much all the other musicians who live in your city. If you haven't played with someone, somebody else you've played with has. It makes for a kind of loosely assembled constellation of musicians, where you can connect all the points to one another if you trace carefully enough.

Though I knew a number of established piano teachers, we had heard great things about him, and I felt an almost paternal desire to help the next generation of teachers coming up. So we started weekly lessons. My son studied with him on and off for about a year. I say "on and off" mainly because his teacher would often cancel his lessons at the last minute. He'd text my wife that he'd forgotten about a rehearsal, or a gig, or a recording session. He was always apologetic, but the message was clear: gigs came before lessons.

As a working musician and teacher myself, I felt that to a certain extent, I understood. Most of us get into this business to *play* first and foremost, and many musicians teach to earn a reliable income to subsidize their playing, which tends to pay very little. On occasion, I will also cancel a lesson to make a gig. So I felt that as a fellow musician, I should cut him some slack. Like so many of us, he was just trying to put it all together and make a living with his music.

As a parent, however, I wanted my son to have some consistency, especially at such a young and impressionable age. I felt it was critical for him to have weekly lessons to stay focused and on track, and to make the progress so vital to enjoying the process. To miss a lesson here or there was no big deal. But to miss two or three out of every five lessons? And to cancel at the last minute—or worse still, to just not show up? We started to think about finding someone more reliable.

But my son was attached to him. This was the first person to teach my son about music who wasn't his parent—someone who introduced him to a whole new world of possibilities on a new instrument and helped him navigate his first real journey outside of familiar and safe territory; someone who gave him well-earned praise and positive feedback, and who could even motivate him to practice without being nagged by his parents. And of course, my son liked hanging and talking music with someone who was hip and cool and wasn't his dad. He always looked forward to his lessons.

Just as my wife and I were contemplating the possibility of making a change, she got a text from his teacher, predictably just before his lesson, canceling again. Apparently, he'd gotten a gig teaching at a local music school. He explained he would be cutting back on his private lessons, and would no longer be able to teach our son. There was no phone call. There was no last lesson. There was no communication with my son. There was no goodbye.

We told our son about it the next day. He tried to hide it as his eyes softened from disbelief to welling up with tears, but in the end he couldn't hold back. He cried. We told him we'd find him a better teacher, one who would show up every week and with whom he'd really get along. But it didn't matter. The damage was done.

My son is passionate about music, and as time has passed, this ultimately registered as a very minor setback, a small bump in the road. But it made me think back to my days as a young drummer and how important the relationship with my teacher was to me. He was a motivator, an adult role model other than my parents, who showed me that people could play music very, very well without necessarily being famous—and make a living pursuing their passion. He also opened a whole world for me and helped me take my first real steps toward becoming the musician I am today.

There are many incredibly talented musicians who teach. However, being a good musician doesn't make you a good teacher. Naturally, you have to have expertise and an in-depth understanding of your instrument—its history, technique, and its role in the music. You also have to be able to explain things in a way that people can understand. And you have to want them to understand. You have to believe there is something special and meaningful in what you do, and take care in how you transmit it to others. You have to recognize that people learn differently; that your role is to help each student reach their potential and open the door to the infinite and transcendent possibilities of music. And you have to recognize that the relationship can have a meaningful impact on their lives.

Sometimes I watch my son play from the corner of the room where he can't see me. As I listen to him, I wonder what role music will play in his life, whether he will experience the same elation and heartache that I do with it. I wonder whether he will grow up to play professionally, and I feel both excited and concerned for him at the same time. But then he turns around to let me know he sees me, a huge smile on his face as he continues to play. And I remember that none of that matters.

TOUGH LOVE

For about a year in my thirties, I taught a student who hardly ever practiced. He had plenty of talent, but was very disorganized; the kind of kid who struggled in school with turning in his assignments. He'd often forget his books and materials and show up to his lessons without his sticks. I tried repeatedly to help him stay on top of things. We'd reorganize his drum binder, try keeping a practice log, set up a schedule for his practice…but none of it seemed to work. Eventually, he stopped taking lessons. We parted amicably, and I even suggested that he see about studying with another teacher just to try something different, and I gave him a couple of recommendations.

A few months later, he called me to let me know he had started taking lessons with a colleague of mine, that it was going well and he was practicing regularly and coming in prepared for his lessons. "Wow," I said. "That's great! What happened to motivate you to start practicing?" "Well," he replied, "I showed up for the first lesson, which went fine, but then I showed up the second week and I hadn't practiced and I had forgotten my books like I used to. But then the teacher told me he wasn't willing to work with me. He said he only works with students who take their drumming seriously, who practice every week and come prepared. He said his time was valuable, and he didn't want to waste it working with students who didn't value his time. So I started practicing. He gave me one more chance, and it's worked out great ever since."

More than anything, I was glad to hear he had gotten on track. It was also a good reminder to me that for some people, tough love is the best kind of caring. In two weeks, my colleague had achieved the positive result with this student that had eluded me for over a year. It made me think I should have taken the same approach early on.

I know this tack doesn't work with everyone. Some students would balk at the stern demand and might quit lessons entirely. I respected my fellow teacher for staying true to his values and for setting clear expectations and limits with his students.

I do believe it's important to set expectations with students at the outset. Generally, the more you expect, the more they rise to meet those expectations. But the truth is it doesn't always work like that, and sometimes you need to be more patient to help people find their motivation and grow into their practice. I know that's what I needed when I was a teenager. And now, as a parent, I can attest that tough love doesn't always do the trick.

YOU'RE ONLY FOOLING YOURSELF

I studied with two different drum teachers before I got to high school. The first one was on the faculty at Julliard. He was patient and encouraging and helped me off to a positive start. I studied with him for a year and a half before he moved away. Soon after, I started up with a grad student of his. I don't remember very much about working with him, except for one particular lesson that has stuck with me my entire life. It wasn't a drum lesson.

For some weeks I had not been practicing, but would lie to my teacher that I had been. As a teacher now, I know this is fairly typical among younger students. We don't want to disappoint our teachers, and we're embarrassed when we haven't been practicing and living up to their—and our own—expectations. So I told him each week that I'd been practicing when I hadn't, and I'd often come up with excuses to my parents as to why I needed to cancel my lesson.

One week, a couple of days after my lesson, I finally decided to crack open my lesson notebook. As it happened, that week my teacher had written a note in my book that read, "If you read this, sign here." He was trying to catch me in a lie, to show me that he knew I wasn't practicing. Instead of feeling good that I'd actually opened my book to practice that week, I felt ashamed. It was clear my teacher knew I hadn't been practicing. I hadn't been fooling him at all...only myself.

I can attest now that 99% of the time, within the first two minutes of every lesson, I can tell whether my students have been practicing, regardless of what they tell me. (Even though I don't always get an honest answer, I do usually ask them how the week of practicing went. I want to make them feel accountable for coming in prepared.) When I sense that my students aren't being truthful, I often relate my story of how I used to lie to my teacher. I tell them that whether they practice or not doesn't have an impact on me, that I already know how to play the drums; that they are here because they decided they wanted to learn and improve, and that telling me the truth actually helps me set my expectations about their progress and helps me determine what to work on at the lesson. Most of all, I explain, lying doesn't make them any better, nor feel better about themselves. Even if I believed them, it wouldn't change the fact that they didn't do the work and didn't make progress.

Occasionally, it gets through. When it doesn't, I remind myself that I was just like them when I was young. And, that part of what I am here to do is teach them to recognize that they are responsible to themselves first and foremost—and that their progress, or lack thereof, is for them to own and to learn from.

DIFFERENT TEACHING AND LEARNING STYLES

Not everybody learns the same way. As self-evident as this seems, there are many teachers who don't consider this in their teaching practices. They teach the same material with the same rigid approach because that's how they learned, and they've been doing it that way forever. If you're lucky, you may find a good fit with a teacher like this. But for the most part, that approach only works with a very particular kind of student who happens to work well with that teacher's style.

I know other teachers who swing to the opposite extreme, whose lessons have little, if any, structure. Their students decide what to work on at each lesson, and often meander from topic to topic, not making any meaningful progress. This kind of approach can also on rare occasion work well, but only with the most self-disciplined of learners.

I think lessons are most effective with a balance of structure and variability. Students need to develop a foundation of musical skills they can apply in a variety of situations, but they also need to be invested in the process by playing the music they like and learning what interests them. Nobody decides they want to be a drummer so they can learn to play double paradiddles—they take up drums mostly because they want to *rock!* (or *swing*, as the case may be).

One of the main benefits of working with a private instructor is that you get personal attention suited to your needs. Despite my structured approach, each student I teach has a personally-tailored program. There is certainly plenty of overlap among them, but no two programs are exactly alike. Some students play in their school symphonic band, so we focus on reading, rolls, and rudiments. Others are preparing for or playing in their high school jazz band or combo, so we'll work on swing, soloing, and chart reading skills. Others participate in the BandWorks program or play in a rock band, so we focus more on grooves and fill vocabulary. My adult students play in a wide range of bands, from rock, blues, jazz, to funk and reggae. I've had middle and high school music directors who wanted to bone up on their percussion chops, one student who only wanted to learn to play avant-garde jazz, students who only wanted to learn brushes, and students who come to work with me on New Orleans second-line playing, one of my specialties.

Even among my beginning students looking for an introduction and a strong foundation, I may take a slightly different approach based on how they learn. Some students are visual learners, while others learn better aurally. Some can pick up my meaning and intention from one sentence, while others need to hear a concept explained several ways to understand it, and will benefit from looking at things from a number of different perspectives. Some students need constant feedback on how they are playing, while others prefer more room to experiment and figure it out for themselves.

There is also a wide range of how quickly students will progress. Certainly the biggest factor is how much they practice, but even with the same amount of quality practice, different students will progress at different rates, relative to their abilities—and require different kinds of support. If I have a student who can come in and nail a snare drum étude with little practice, I might challenge her to play it with more dynamics, or to increase the tempo (and I'll always suggest that if she can play it that well with little practice, she should see what she could do when she really applies herself to it). Conversely, if a student comes in and has worked hard at the same piece but made only modest progress, that may be a bigger achievement, relatively speaking, and I will support it as such.

Not every drummer will achieve the same heights of skill or proficiency, but all will improve with work and dedication. For most students, the improvement is the important thing. The more talented and dedicated the student, the harder I'll push them.

I like to encourage a student's strengths while shoring up their weaknesses. If I have a student who has an incredible ear, I may sit down to play things and ask him to play them back, or record myself playing exercises I want him to learn to play. But we will also focus a lot on his reading, and work on transcribing. Likewise, if I have a good reader (many classical musicians come in as good readers but very tentative improvisers), we will focus more on playing by ear and improvising. If a teacher treats every student exactly the same, that teacher can miss important opportunities—often the most critical ones—to help them grow and succeed.

LEARNING ISSUES

I don't believe that some people "have no rhythm." Certain people will need to work harder than others to get to the same point, and, naturally, people will learn at different rates. Some people may have a more attuned innate sense of rhythm and timing, but everyone can learn to develop it—and the people who go far are the ones who work hardest at it, not necessarily the ones who are quickest on the uptake.

Though I have no formal training in working with people with learning disabilities, I have worked with a number of students, both kids and adults, who have both diagnosed and undiagnosed learning issues. I had one student who was extremely smart and intuitive, but for the life of him, could not read triplet swing patterns. I had another who could play back anything by ear perfectly on the first try, but couldn't reliably remember the difference between a quarter note and an eighth note despite repeated efforts to learn to read. I've had students who struggled mightily to find the pulse in a song. I even worked with a bass player once who had an incredible ear and a great pocket, but didn't even know the names of the notes he was playing. Ask him to play a "G" and he'd ask you to play it first so he could find it.

People come to me with a range of learning strengths and weaknesses. I do my best to recognize them, learn about them through experimentation and a little outside research, and try to teach in a way to help these students most effectively. Sometimes a diagnosis of dyslexia or ADHD can proffer a strategy. For example, I might teach someone with ADHD in short mini-lessons, with frequent breaks within the arc of a longer lesson (although some people with ADHD can focus like a laser on something that interests them).

Or I might come up with alternative, onomatopoeic verbalizations (think "choc-late-shake, wa-ter-mel-on, french-fry," and such) for people who struggle with the standard 16th note counting system.

Occasionally learning difficulties show up in different fashions, manifesting in ways sometimes even the student didn't know about until they started drumming. I have one such student I've been working with for the past four years.

This student (I'll call her Katy) is one of the most perceptive musicians I've ever taught. She goes out to hear live music every week and comes back with wonderfully astute observations about the drummers she hears. We have great conversations about music in general and about drumming specifically. Katy's understanding and awareness of the role of the drummer is as sophisticated as mine, and she speaks with a wisdom well beyond her years of experience. Katy can play simple patterns and has learned to read at an advanced-beginner level, but her playing vocabulary is extremely limited, and she has trouble with aural processing.

Over the course of the years, we've tried all sorts of experiments to help her: we've played in the pitch dark to help sharpen her listening skills; we've done copycat exercises where she'll try to play back what I played; we've slowed things way down and looped them using a software program; worked hard on developing hand speed; and tried everything from reading written patterns along with the metronome to meditating and playing free, without judgment. We usually make some progress, and she maintains a positive attitude all the time, happy to be playing and working at it. Though our efforts often fail to bear much fruit, occasionally we'll hit on something that really resonates with her and helps her move through some challenge. Most importantly, we both enjoy the process of digging deeper to figure out what works for her and what doesn't.

THE DRUMMING BRAIN

Neuroscientists have known for decades that each half of the brain is responsible for controlling the motor coordination of one half of the body. The left half of the brain, in addition to being primarily responsible for analytical, logical, and mathematical thinking, is responsible for the motor coordination of the right side of the body. The right half of the brain, thought to be the origin of creativity, language, and artistry, controls the left half of the body.

Drumming, especially drum set playing, is a unique endeavor. To do it well requires detailed analysis and mathematical understanding, but also creativity and artistry—a unique combination of both halves of the brain. Furthermore, it requires the integration of both sides of the body, using all four limbs in orchestrated synchronicity.

The brain is made up of about 100 billion neurons. Every time a drummer learns a new coordination pattern, she creates new pathways in her neuronal network. The more pathways a drummer creates, the easier it becomes to make new ones which are similar to the old.

Drummer jokes abound in the music community. Some of them are actually funny. They mostly have a common theme, which supports the stereotype that drummers are not smart, or at least not as smart as other musicians. After all, they don't need to understand music theory, don't need to know scales or harmony, and, in many cases, don't know how to read music (though that's true of many other musicians too).

Though it's true that drummers don't *need* to know as much music theory as most other musicians, most professional drummers actually do. Most also play a number of other instruments, including piano, guitar, and sometimes winds and brass. Most accomplished drummers I know are *extremely* smart and are often high achievers in other disciplines as well.

There have been a number of scientific articles published on research of drummers' brains, including one by the Karolinska

Institutet in Sweden, which found a link between intelligence, good timing, and the part of the brain used for problem-solving. It turned out that the most proficient drummers in their study also scored the highest on a problem-solving set unrelated to music. Which only confirms what I already knew: drumming makes you smarter.

COMPETENCE AND CONFIDENCE

Confidence is the belief that one can do something well consistently. This belief in one's ability in turn comes from the experience of doing it consistently. And that experience comes from practice. So, for the most part, practice fosters consistency, which in turn creates competence, which breeds confidence.

But not always. I have some students, mostly younger ones, who have no fear whatsoever about getting up on stage and smacking the drums like they're playing a vicious game of whack-a-mole, even if they can barely play or keep time. It doesn't even occur to them that they should shy away from putting themselves out there 100%. Play a five-minute drum solo in front of a huge crowd even though they know only know a couple of rock beats? No problem!

I have other, mostly adult students who have reasonable facility and can keep a good groove, but who are absolutely petrified to perform on stage. They gently tap the drums as if they were trying not to disturb anyone, even in the privacy of their lessons. Suggest they play a fill at a certain spot and they turn red in the face and suggest they'll work on it at home.

Generally, it's much easier to teach competence than confidence. When a student comes in brimming with confidence, I always am supportive of it, knowing how difficult it can be to cultivate. We work on raising the level of proficiency to be more in line with that self-assuredness, so it's a confidence backed up by skill and not bravado.

When a student's confidence is lacking or negatively dispro-portionate to their actual ability, we work on exercises to develop trust in their playing. These can be really fun (at least for me—the students are often terrified to try them). I'll encourage them to meditate on something they do really well and already have confidence in, and try to channel that feeling into their playing. Sometimes we'll work on *not trying* to play anything, but just playing whatever comes to mind with no judgment, suspending the expectation of sounding good. Other times I'll find recordings for them to play along with that don't have any drums on them, so there is nothing to compare to, or try to emulate. Without holding their parts up for comparison, it's remarkable how much better they can feel about their playing.

A lot of adults have baggage about performing from when they were kids. A piano recital gone awry, a mean teacher, an overly strict parent who never praised their effort, an embarrassing moment of humiliation in front of people; or, among some of the younger generation, parents who tell them that everything they play is incredible and that they're god's gift to the world. All these things can create anxiety for people that they sometimes need to address in order to move past it. I joke with some of my students and fellow teachers that *half of my job is drum instructor, the other half therapist*. As a teacher, I try to help my students develop competence. And as a therapist, I try to help those who struggle with it to gain confidence.

HOW TO KNOW IF YOU'RE "GOOD"

This may sound funny, but for a few years in my twenties, I had a complex about knowing how "good" I was. I'd compare myself to just about every drummer I heard, and, in the process, ensure that I didn't listen to or really enjoy what I was hearing, since my mind was so busy with comparisons. I'd imagine many different levels of drummer and wanted very much to know where I stood in the scheme of things. Looking back now, I can attribute this to immaturity and insecurity.

One of my favorite sayings at the archery club where I shoot is: "You is who you was before you got here." If you're struggling on a given day, you had that struggle in you. If you're excelling on a given day, you had that in you too. We're capable of a range of quality of performance, and there is no denying that how you perform is a true indicator of what you were capable of on a given day, under all the given circumstances. There's little use in getting hung up on making comparisons. You can only control the things within your control. If you're hungry to get better, go and practice. Over time, you will improve.

Many musicians seek validation of some kind when they play. They might look for a compliment from their fellow musicians, or their teacher, or band director. They want to be perceived as being "good," whatever that means. And even though getting praise feels great, my advice to drummers is to focus on making the best music they can. All you can do is prepare well, pour your effort and heart into making your music, and derive satisfaction from knowing you gave it everything you had. It doesn't mean you're not eager to get better, or make better music—just that on that gig, on that day, on that song, in that moment, you did the best you could. Conversely, if you mailed in a performance or didn't prepare as well as you could have, does it really feel good to get a compliment when you know you didn't put forth your best?

Duke Ellington sagely said, "If it sounds good and it feels good, it is good." It really is that simple. It doesn't matter what level you are, or who you're playing with, whether it's in your living room or at an arena full of 50,000 people. If it sounded good and felt good to you, it's a pretty good indication that you made some worthwhile music.

A CRISIS OF CONFIDENCE/THE GUITAR WHISPERER

During a lesson, I sometimes trade seats with my students, sit down at the kit, and play the same beat my student is playing, at the same tempo. I'll ask them if it sounds any different. It always does. "What sounds different about it?" I ask. "It sounds better," they say. "Why? What makes it sound better to your ears?" I question. I try to get them thinking about the quality of the overall sound they create, the tones of the individual drums and cymbals, the relative dynamic balance of the parts of the kit, and the consistency with which they play it. If that doesn't work, I'll ask leading questions to try to get them to think critically and come up with some ideas. "Does my hi-hat sound the same as yours?" I'll query. "How loud was my snare drum compared to yours?" "Was I leaving the bass drum beater in the head or letting it rebound?" And so on.

One thing that they always remark is that I play with more confidence. "Sure," I allow. "What if I asked you to play with that same confidence? What would stop you from sounding more confident?"

At this point in a lesson I like to try an experiment: I'll ask them to take a minute to think about some other thing they do in their lives that they feel very confident doing. For adults, it could be whatever they do vocationally: crunch numbers, write code, give speeches, cook, cut hair, fix cars, practice law, or even something as simple as driving. For kids, it's usually a subject in school that they excel at, or a sport or hobby that they like. It doesn't really matter, except that it's something they don't think about when they do it— they just do it, and they are confident in their ability without feeling self-conscious about it.

Once they decide on something, I'll ask them to take a minute to get into the headspace they're in when they're engaged with this activity. "Imagine you're about to bake that batch of cookies, and you know they're going to taste great. You are going to *rock* those cookies, and you're confident and excited to eat them and share them with your friends. It doesn't even occur to you to doubt yourself. Now sit with that feeling for a few seconds...then play that drum beat like you're going to bake those cookies."

A lot of the time, I really do hear a difference in their playing.

I tried this one time in a different context. I worked as the drummer and musical director/coach for a band of lawyers at a multinational law firm. They had an in-house band that would play at the firm's holiday parties and partner retreats. It was a great group of people and a lot of fun. As high-powered attorneys and amateur musicians, they really relished the opportunities to play, and it was fun to be around that enthusiasm.

We were rehearsing at a venue just before the gig. The guitarist had a solo intro to a song, a two-bar pickup. He would play it correctly some of the time, so it was clear he was capable of nailing it. Other times he would stumble, and his execution would be problematic for the band's entrance, as we needed him to establish the time in the intro. I sensed his anxiety about playing it right, and that he recognized that the band was relying on him. During a break, I pulled him aside with his guitar.

"What's going on in your head when you play that riff?" I asked. He answered something about his unease with not knowing each time whether he would pull it off. I suggested that his anxiety about screwing it up might be what was causing him to muff it. "I've heard you play it correctly dozens of times. You are totally capable of playing it right, and playing it right consistently," I said. Then I asked him to imagine he was doing some kind of lawyer thing he did every day with great confidence and ease (I didn't really know what to go for, but he got the picture). He took a minute. I saw his face relax, in contrast to the frustrated countenance he'd displayed a moment before. He played the lick. And he nailed it. He nailed it again a half-hour later on the gig too.

One of the other band members had been eavesdropping on our discussion. "You're the guitar whisperer," he said. I smiled at the compliment, and put a finger to my lips. "Shh," I said.

VERSE 1

Honing a Practice

CHOOSE YOUR BATTLES

I know some teachers who give their students things that are very challenging to play mainly for the sake of their being difficult. This makes no sense to me. There is no shortage of valuable things to work on, with plenty of difficulty to go around. We all have a limited amount of time to practice and explore the various topics that interest us. Why waste it on things just because they're challenging?

The more you know, the more you realize how little you actually know. There is just such depth of knowledge, understanding, and facility that is possible in even very narrow disciplines. This is why experts tend to specialize so much. It can take a lifetime to learn not just drumming, but something as specific as Nigerian batá drumming or New Orleans second-line drumming.

Given the infinite scope and breadth of drumming topics, you should spend the vast majority of your precious practice time working on things that help you achieve your goals, not on things that just happen to be difficult.

WHAT YOU PRACTICE VS. WHAT YOU PLAY

Many musicians don't have clear ideas about the steps they need to take in order to achieve a certain goal, if they have any goals at all. Frequently, students will espouse a vague notion of wanting to "be better," without any real idea of what that means. Maybe they have an interest in heavy metal or jazz, but often it doesn't get much more specific than a style of music they like.

If there's music that turns you on, that's great. If you want to learn to play it, however, you need to determine which skill sets you need to develop in order to do it. Every style of music has its own particular coordination patterns, idioms, and vocabulary, and requires a certain range of touch and feel. Some of those building blocks can only be acquired by working on very mechanical skills (for example, in order to play heavy metal, you need to work on developing very fast double bass drum speed), while others are more conceptual (for example, the notion that bebop comping tends to be phrased around upbeat punctuations).

Either way, everything I teach my students has a utilitarian value. Most of the time it will be plainly evident why an exercise or skill set is relevant, but sometimes certain aspects of their facility development will have a less obvious or immediate application. When an athlete trains, she works on many drills specific to her sport, but also on general conditioning which enables her to use her body's potential to its fullest capabilities. She may also work on balance, coordination, and flexibility—things that will clearly be helpful, but may not seem as directly germane to the novice athlete. Similarly, a drummer should work on sticking, rudiments, posture, stroke, etc. These things help drummers play more easily and efficiently.

For several years, I've taken my son fishing on an annual summer vacation up to a lake in the Sierras. Each year my son would be excited to go spend quality time with me on a boat for a couple of hours, and I relished the time with him out in nature, away from the distractions of cell phones and computer screens. The only problem was, for years we didn't catch a fish. Not one.

To be honest, we didn't really know what we were doing. For the first couple of years, we were using the wrong bait. Then we spent some time with the wrong set up and fishing at the wrong depth. Later we learned that fish tend to feed mostly at certain times of the day. There have always been plenty of fish in that lake, evidenced by all the people we'd see coming back with several fish to show for their efforts. We'd even see people catching them, then float over nearby to try and fish close to the "good spot." Still nothing.

Finally, this past summer, after seven unsuccessful fishing trips, we caught our first fish. (OK, he caught it. I'm still getting skunked.) It was a spectacular rainbow trout. Even more spectacular was the huge smile on his face. As he was reeling it in, it occurred to me that if we were out to catch a fish, what we should've been doing all along was learning *how* to fish. Fishing was fun to be sure, but while we were fishing, we weren't expanding our knowledge and understanding of how to fish very effectively. Sure, we got to practice casting, and you could say that each time we went out we learned something new. But most of what we learned we could have picked up far more quickly had we done some research, as opposed to just venturing out uninformed trying to catch a fish.

Knowledge, technique, real life experience...all are essential. If you skip the knowledge and technique and just practice fishing (or drumming as the case may be) without really knowing what you're doing, it's going to be a long, slow process, and you won't catch nearly as many fish. 'Cuz fishing is fun, but catching fish is more fun.

WHAT PRACTICING ISN'T

At my teaching studio, I have a neighbor who plays drums in the studio next door. I can hear him through the wall playing every weekday. He doesn't play along with music, and he doesn't really practice. He plays mostly the same routine, recycling the grooves and fills he knows, and "jams" for about four hours. Every day. He doesn't get perceptibly better, and he never works on anything new. No dynamics either. Always full blast. I find this dumbfounding. And it drives me crazy.

Anybody who has that kind of time to play ought to spend a good chunk of it practicing, or working on *getting better*. Some drummers unfortunately think that playing and practicing are the same thing. They aren't.

Practicing means working, generally on things you're not yet good at. Sure, it's important to keep your chops up with grooves or rudiments that may already be familiar. You are never done practicing the fundamentals. However, that's not the same thing as adding new skills or songs to your repertoire.

A sax player I know told me that when he was attending the Berklee College of Music in Boston, he'd walk down the hallway lined with practice rooms and hear students tearing it up. What were they working on? Clearly they'd had to practice to get there, but apparently they would choose to spend most of their time playing what they already knew. Generally, you're not supposed to sound good when you're practicing, at least not when you're learning something new. The goal of practicing is to refine technique, increase vocabulary, and explore creativity—and to develop new musical tools and learn how to use them. That takes practice, and some time spent not sounding great, at least in the beginning.

THE SPIRAL OF PRACTICING

A significant part of my job as a teacher is to help motivate my students to practice. Most teachers I know who have a robust teaching practice share my experience of having a small number of highly motivated and dedicated students, a large number of students who practice a moderate amount, and small number who struggle either to make the time or find the motivation. Often I tell these students that inertia can be the most challenging thing to overcome. When students don't practice, they come to their lessons and work on the same material every week. They feel badly about themselves for not practicing and not progressing despite the best of their intentions. They go home feeling embarrassed and overwhelmed by how far behind they are, which makes them feel even less like practicing. It's a self-sustaining cycle of negativity. I see it a lot.

Conversely, when students practice regularly, they come in to their lessons excited to demonstrate how much progress they've made. They get validating feedback on their hard work, and feel energized and inspired to continue to develop their skills. They look forward to their lessons. The better they get, the more motivated they are to keep getting better.

I try to tell those who are struggling with motivation that it's possible to get into the positive practice spiral, that the toughest thing is getting over the inertia of not practicing at all. Instead of worrying about the big picture, they should start with committing to practicing *one time*. Then another...and another. After one or two successful practices in a week, I try to get them to commit to practicing three times, and establish a foundation upon which to build. I've found that it takes at least three practices for a student to make meaningful progress with something—I'm not talking about mastery, but just enough improvement to notice and feel good about. From there, we shoot for adding more practices on top of that baseline. A journey of 10,000 miles begins with one step. And you can only take one step at a time, after all.

ENJOYING WHERE YOU ARE

Regardless of where you are on your path of drumming (or music, or writing, or sports, or whatever discipline you're engaged in), it's important to enjoy the process. So many of my students are fixated on arriving *at some place. They ask me questions like "How long will it take me to get good?" Or "How long until I can play like John Bonham from Led Zeppelin?" Though these questions are naïve—they are of course the "wrong" questions, demonstrating a lack of appreciation, humility, and understanding of the process— they do however demonstrate a desire. So rather than dismiss them as the immature and impulsive "get me there quick" attitudes of the young, I try to take them in stride.*

I had a friend in college who could fingerpick and sing the Bob Dylan song, "Mama, You've Been on My Mind." I had just started playing guitar, and I thought it was the coolest sounding thing ever. When I heard him play it for the first time, I told him then and there that if I could learn to do that, I would never need to learn anything else to be a happy and satisfied guitar player for the rest of my life. Several months later, I was playing it as well as my friend who'd been playing guitar for several years. And though I was happy to be able to play it, never for a moment did I think I had "arrived." Naturally, I was hungry for more.

And so it goes. There is no destination in music, only the journey. As much as you know and as good as you may be, there is always more to learn and appreciate. That's one of the best things about music—the deeper you dig, the richer the treasure. *And no matter how good you get, there will always be plenty of people out there who can play better than you can (and of course, music is not a competitive sport). There is no finish line, no arrival, no certificate you get for Being Good. Every time you achieve one goal, another one crops up on your horizon.*

In all my years of teaching, I've found that the students who achieve the most are the ones who enjoy it the most, regardless of where they are. Ninety-five percent of my students haven't gone on to pursue careers in music. And the ones who have are not necessarily the happiest. Enjoy the process. It's all there is.

I played in a band for a few years with a keyboard player who, at every set break and after every gig, would talk about all the things the band didn't do right, all the mistakes that were made and the ways in which the music wasn't perfect. At first I was all ears, and would engage with processing what we could have done better. After all, we were all there to make the music sound as good as we could, and it seemed logical to analyze and evaluate what went wrong. But after enough gigs like this, it started to grow tiresome. There was never any appreciation of what went right, no acknowledgment of the great energy we played with—really nothing positive at all. I began to dread the gigs and the inevitable deprecating tirades that would follow. I realized that this person was working out his own self-doubts surrounding his music, and the self-flagellation was driven by his ego. Once I realized what was happening, I quit the band and never looked back.

It's important to always strive to improve. For me that's part of the fun—just like trying to lower my golf score (and I'll admit, I am a competitive person when it comes to sports and games). But if you're not enjoying the journey, you're at risk of missing what playing music is all about. I've found this to be true at all levels of musicianship, from the rank beginner to the seasoned professional. Try not to take yourself too seriously, and appreciate where you are. You'll enjoy playing more. It might even help you play better.

THRESHOLD PRACTICING

There is nothing more discouraging than working hard at something and not improving. I've known a number of drummers who spin their wheels in frustration working on various aspects of their playing, only to make incremental progress toward their goals. I have seen some drummers quit playing for this very reason. And who wouldn't? If you feel like you're working hard but not getting anywhere, it's easy to lose your motivation and resolve.

Why? How could it be that you spend time practicing and not improving? Doesn't practice make perfect? Isn't that how you get to Carnegie Hall?

It's not just how much you practice, but also how you practice that matters.

Many amateur drummers, exasperated by their lack of progress, spend much of their time practicing sloppily and often don't realize it. They stumble and struggle, getting good at making mistakes by repeating the same inaccuracies again and again. In self-diagnosing their problems, they take the wrong medicine for their ailments, or the right medicine in too-small doses, instead of working on the right things for longer periods of time. Understandably aggravated, they tend to lose focus and patience very easily, moving on to the next thing before they've mastered the first.

An attentive teacher can offer unbiased feedback about how things sound and where they need improvement. And, most importantly, a teacher can impart to her students an understanding of how to practice effectively.

When you're trying to learn a new physical move—especially one as challenging as a four-limbed coordination pattern on the drums—your brain needs time to figure out the correct neural pathways to send complex sequences of impulses to various parts of the body. When you don't execute exactly what you intended, it usually means there was a glitch somewhere along the way, a short circuit that caused a part of the body to fire at the wrong time, or to *not* move precisely when it was supposed to. *Pay attention to the signals your body gives you about how it learns.* Most of the time, you just need to slow down to allow more time—sometimes even just a fraction of a second—to perform the move as you intended it.

Trying harder doesn't usually yield better results either. Focused concentration and visualization can certainly increase the likelihood of success, but if you're going too fast, it doesn't matter how hard you try to concentrate.

Most people know when they make mistakes. However, instead of slowing down to play more accurately, they just keep trying again at the same speed, usually making the same error over and over. As you execute a move repeatedly in the same manner, your brain begins to create something called *myelin sheathing* around the activated neurons. Much like insulation around wires, this sheathing helps the brain transmit signals with less energy loss along the way. The more a pattern is reiterated the same way, the more efficiently the brain transmits the impulse to continue to be able to execute the task consistently, whether it's being played as intended or not. Thus, the more times you imprint the same unintentional mistake, the more difficult it becomes to unlearn it; the more you play it right, the easier it becomes to continue playing it right.

During lessons, I'll ask my students why they think they are stumbling and what they need to do in order to teach themselves to play something correctly. Many of them know that I'm going to tell them to slow down, so they volunteer, reflexively: "I need to slow down." And then they proceed to play at exactly the same tempo at which they just faltered. Others will slow down, and still make mistakes—they need to go slower still. Occasionally students will have difficulty slowing down enough because they are embarrassed at the need to play something so slowly, as if it were a judgment on their ability. I encourage students to let go of any expectations about how something is supposed to sound and not to think of it as a musical exercise for a moment. This allows them to learn it without the inherent judgment that it isn't sounding good yet.

Every musician can play whatever she can play, up to a certain tempo, beyond which the playing becomes less accurate and inconsistent (i.e., less controlled). No matter how good the player or how facile the exercise or passage, naturally it can only be played up to some threshold tempo before it breaks down.

• When you're trying to get faster at something, the optimum practice speed is *just below* your threshold speed. It should feel slightly challenging, but still in control and *consistently correct*. It's like skiing—if you go a little too fast, you feel just barely in control, and it's impossible to work on your form. With drumming, when you surpass the threshold, you start practicing sloppily.

• Your goal is *accurate* repetitions. Repeating the correct execution ingrains the pattern in your nervous system and also allows your ear to pick up on how it's supposed to sound. Your ear can help you learn very effectively. It's so much easier to pick something up if you hear it correctly over and over, as opposed to hearing the wrong thing, or something that keeps changing every time; it's as if your ear doesn't know which version of it to latch onto to try to repeat.

- The more consistently accurate your playing is, the faster you'll learn. Aim for an accuracy rate above 90%. If you can achieve that, it will quickly rise to above 95%, and ultimately approach 100%.

- The more you practice just below your threshold tempo, the more comfortable that slightly challenging speed becomes. Over time, you become able to bump up the maximum threshold, and correspondingly, the "just below threshold" tempo increases too. So you can get faster without ever actually trying to force it past your limit. On the flip side, you can practice much slower than your threshold tempo, and that can be effective too.

- As your threshold rises, you will increase your dexterity and speed, sometimes even in the course of a few minutes. However, the progress is not always linear. Just because you can play 16th notes evenly at 200 beats per minute one day doesn't mean you'll necessarily be able to do it the next, especially if that speed is close to your threshold. You'll have good days and bad, and as you improve, your worst days will get better and better.

On rare occasions, I run into students who can play a groove or exercise better at a faster tempo than they can at a more relaxed pace. Sometimes, for example, a drummer can get comfortable playing a double 16th note bass drum figure at a very fast speed, but when they try to play it slower, they struggle to relax the fast-twitch of their muscles to put more space between the notes. I remind these students that they don't want to be the kind of drummer who has to play at a particular tempo to play well; that if slower is less controlled, it means that they need to spend more time practicing to become equally comfortable at a wide range of tempos.

The quickest, most direct path to being able to play something faster is almost always to play it slower.

BREAKING IT DOWN

After going too fast, the most common reason students experience difficulty with a part is because they are trying to perform too many operations at one time. They attempt to play a complex groove with multiple elements when they haven't mastered the basic building blocks, or they try to play a longer passage when they haven't mastered the smaller pieces of it.

In all my years of teaching, I have never had a student who couldn't play a simple rock beat with all four limbs working simultaneously by the end of the first lesson. How is that possible? Because we break it down into small pieces that anybody can learn. We start with one limb at a time, playing on certain beats out of a four-count, then start pairing them together two at a time in various combinations, then three at a time, and eventually all four. Before you know it, you're playing a full rock beat on the drum set with all four limbs working in concert.

However, if I showed new students this same rock beat and played it for them, and even broke it down to explain how each limb moves, very few of them would be able to play it outright. You have to teach your body in smaller steps, one piece at a time.

In competitive target archery (the kind they shoot at the Olympics), the apparently simple endeavor of shooting an arrow is broken down into 12 separate steps, collectively referred to as the *shot cycle*, each with its own nuances. Elite level archers will work on each of these 12 steps, deconstructing them into the smallest and most subtle micro-movements in order to achieve consistency and repeatability. This technique of isolating smaller, specific aspects of a larger, more complex move, is a critical component to effective practicing.

If I could only give two pieces of advice to help students learn to practice more effectively, they would be: *slow it down* and *break it down*.

WORKING ON ONE THING AT A TIME

A guitar teacher friend who was teaching in the studio next door to me one day remarked after a lesson I'd taught, that he heard me working with one of my students on a single drum fill for over half an hour. It was the intro fill into the groove on Led Zeppelin's "Good Times, Bad Times." He couldn't believe how long we'd stuck with it. "It was a really challenging fill," I replied.

I find that students often lack the discipline to work long enough on whatever they're practicing, be it a groove, a fill, a snare drum étude or sticking exercise. Eager to get to the next thing, they tend to rush through a limited number of repetitions, forgetting that mastery is the goal.

Many students treat an exercise like a math problem: they work on it until they "solve" it. Certainly, the first part of working on a new pattern is deciphering it and getting it to the point where you can play it accurately and precisely. But the best and most effective practice doesn't even begin until you can play consistently. That's when muscle memory really starts to kick in, and the body can execute without the brain needing to concentrate so hard. It starts to become second nature, familiar, and starts to *flow*. You can then turn your attention to more subtle aspects like touch and timbre, breath and stroke. Alas, it's very difficult to achieve this level of comfort and facility without *time spent*. Unfortunately, many people don't have the patience to sit with anything long enough for this process to take hold.

You'll be amazed how much more effective your practice will be if you work on less material but practice it more. If a student doesn't have enough time to get to everything over the course of a week, I'd prefer to have her come in and show me one or two things that are meaningfully improved, rather than show me a whole batch of stuff only incrementally better. It's so much more satisfying to have something to show for your effort all week, even if it's only improving on one thing—at least you have something you can put into the bank!

During his lessons, the famous jazz drummer Tony Williams used to insist that his students master whatever they were working on *during the lesson* before he would allow them to move on. While this seems impractical to me and too rigid of an approach, I understand the sentiment behind his method. He wanted his students to really *learn* something and walk away from the lesson having qualitatively improved. In his role as teacher and expert, he used his authority to make sure that they learned.

Like Tony, I find that my students will focus on an exercise or passage for longer during their lessons than they will on their own, and I will use that opportunity to help them get over the hump with it—and in doing so, also show them how much effort some moves may require to master. By the end of the lesson, my student was nailing that John Bonham fill.

After working on something for a long enough period of time, you'll often experience a feeling of it "just clicking." It's like you finally got rid of the little pebble in your shoe, and all of a sudden it feels good and easy to play and requires much less effort. The more you practice effectively, the more you will start to recognize this feeling when it happens, and (hopefully) the more patient you will become in your effort to reach it, because you know the great-feeling reward that awaits you.

That feeling can be elusive, and it can be frustrating when things don't click, despite all your efforts. I find that sometimes getting into the right frame of mind can help. When I'm frustrated trying to nail a linear David Garibaldi groove or a tricky rudimental passage in a Charles Wilcoxon solo, I find that the more frustrated I get, the worse I play it. Good feel comes from relaxed playing, and *tension is the enemy of groove.* So I take a deep breath and refocus, or I come back to it later. Sit with one thing at a time when you practice, and be patient. The deeper you go, the more you'll have to show for it.

WHEN GOING SLOW ISN'T A GOOD THING

There is wisdom in moving slowly when learning something new. There are so many nuances involved in learning a new physical skill. All too frequently, people think they understand something better than they do, and they insist on moving quickly or on to the next step when they have not fully understood or mastered the first. At best, this temporarily slows their progress. At worst, they end up building their skill set on a weak foundation and need to work harder to undo the faults in their technique or approach.

Part of a teacher's job is to figure out how to communicate what each student needs to hear in order to help him or her achieve a desired result. However, this is not to suggest that a teacher should talk too much. There's no easier way to frustrate a student than by having a teacher talk for too long and not allow them to try to apply the concept being taught or use the instruction being offered.

Several summers ago, my then 7-year old attended a one-week golf camp for kids. I was all excited to get him into golf, since I'm an avid player, and I wanted to be able to share the experience of playing golf together as he grew older. I dropped him off at the camp at the local course and decided to stick around to see if I might be able to pick up any tips on how to work with him effectively by watching the instructor.

For the first part of the three-hour camp, the kids sat inside the clubhouse while the instructor talked to them. He went over the rules of the golf range, speaking very slowly. He handed out a sheet that had the rules on it then proceeded to read it aloud after they had already reviewed them. It took an hour. It was painful, and I could see all of the kids start to glaze over and drift off after the first 5–10 minutes. I stuck around for the whole time, and was astounded at the lack of awareness the teacher had that the 10 kids in his charge had stopped paying attention to him 45 minutes before he stopped talking. I could have explained those rules to the kids—even demonstrated them on the driving range—in 10 minutes, thoroughly enough to make sure the kids understood. Once the camp got started in earnest it went a little better, but the instructor still talked too much and didn't let the kids swing or putt enough. My son didn't like the camp and stuck out the week only because we forced him to. In the end, he did learn some decent fundamentals. However, he could have learned a lot more.

The more you have fun doing something, the better you're going to learn it; there's nothing better to help you focus than enthusiasm and hunger to learn. Going slow is usually a good thing, but not always.

THE METRONOME

What a fantastic and infuriating invention is the metronome. There is no better tool for teaching musicians to play in time, or for revealing weaknesses in timing. All musicians should practice at least some of the time with a metronome. Even singers.

I don't start students out with a metronome right away—it's too distracting from this new multidimensional endeavor they are trying to learn, which requires their full concentration. As they get more comfortable, they can begin to pay more attention to things on the periphery of their awareness.

When I do introduce the metronome, I start with something very simple, such as playing single strokes, right and left, one stroke per click. From there we move to 8th notes and 16th notes, dividing each beat into halves and then fourths. After that, we'll work on sticking exercises and reading with the click, as well as rock beats and especially fills, which most drummers tend to rush.

Over time, as students begin to get comfortable keeping time with the click at different tempos, I start testing them by only having them refer to the click once per bar instead of every beat (using a metronome app, you can mute any of the beats in the bar). When they can consistently land on "one," I have them try looking at it only once every two bars. Then every four. I challenge them to see how long they can go keeping time—in their head, or with their hands, feet, or fingers—and still come back on the beat. It's a great exercise that really helps drummers build confidence in their timekeeping.

There are many effective ways to use the metronome and integrate it into your practice. I can honestly say that far more important than *how* you use it is just *that* you use it. I tell my students that they should have the metronome turned on at least some of the time they are practicing, preferably more than half.

If you are going into the studio, you'd better be able to play along with a click. Since most music requires multi-tracking (with the exception of jazz, which is almost always recorded live in the studio), a drummer will need to be able to play along with a click track in order to ensure that the drum tracks are steady for future overdubbing of other instruments. Some Broadway pit orchestras even play along with a click track, since the singers often depend upon specific tempos for the pacing of the lyrics.

A lot of students come to me and tell me they want to improve their time. I always ask them how often they practice or play with a metronome. Usually, the answer is never. There's a simple solution: start by spending 10 minutes a day practicing with a metronome. It doesn't even matter much what you do. Play grooves, fills, and exercises. Improvise. Do it with a click, and do it at a different tempo each day. Your time will improve very quickly, and you'll also learn about your tendencies to rush or drag certain things at different tempos.

THE FIRST SONG

At some point within the first two to three months of teaching a beginning student, we will start working on our first song. Some teachers start students on songs even earlier, but I like to give my students time to develop some vocabulary, get comfortable changing between beats, and play some simple fills. I also want to give them a chance to begin to develop their time feel.

I'll typically choose something simple and on the slower side, but it depends on the student. I like "(Sitting on the) Dock of the Bay" by Otis Redding, "Drive My Car" by the Beatles, "And it Stoned Me" by Van Morrison, or "Back in Black" by AC/DC, but I don't limit it to these. We listen to the song for a bit, and I show them the basic groove. Then I ask them to start playing along with the music, just keeping time, to get a sense of what it feels like to play along with a recording.

Some students are able to do this well on the first try. The beat is comfortable enough and they can pay attention to the music so that they're able to stay in time. For other students, it's very challenging. These students are more or less at the same developmental stage; it's not that some are just "better." The key difference between those who succeed with this and those who struggle at first is where they focus their attention. Or, to put it more plainly, whether they *listen* or not.

To play along with music, live or recorded, you have to be able to multitask, to play a (sometimes complex) coordination pattern on the drums while at the same time focusing your attention outwardly. For my students who struggle with this, the first thing I make sure of is that they can play the beat comfortably. If they have that down, we try listening to the music without playing, counting "1-2-3-4" out loud along with the music. Almost everybody can recognize where the pulse is in the song, but not everyone can tell where the downbeat is. So we start by working on recognizing the "1." We listen for chord changes, vocal phrases, root notes in the bass guitar, and bass drum and snare drum placement. Usually people can find the downbeat within a few minutes. (To test this, I'll start and stop the song at random places and ask them to start counting along as soon as they think they know where the beat is. It's a great listening exercise.) Once they can find the count well enough, we go back to trying to play along, but I ask them to count along as they play.

Another hurdle to playing along with music is that students will sometimes play too loudly. They can focus on the music just fine, feel the tempo and play the part, but they play so loud that they can't hear whether they are locked in with the music or not. They just need to play softer. If they aren't yet able to play with any dynamic control, I may ask them to choke up on the sticks, or use Hot Rods (sticks made out of bundled dowels). This is no excuse to not learn to play with dynamic control, it's just a temporary quick fix so they can play along in time with the music. I remind them that if they can't hear the music, it's impossible to know whether they are playing in time with the band.

There are other intermediary steps you can take to learn to play in time with music, like trying to keep time with just your hi-hat, then adding in the rest of the groove. But usually once a student learns how to focus their attention, they get it fairly quickly. And there's little more satisfying—or important—to a drummer than playing *in time*.

THE RIGHT SIDE/LEFT SIDE EXERCISE

Try this: tap your right foot and your right hand together, once, at the same time. Then tap your left foot and your left hand together one time. Now start alternating, right side then left side. Try to speed up and see how fast you can go until the simultaneity of each side starts to break down. Most people, even non-drummers, can do this at a fairly fast pace.

Now try this: tap your right hand and your left foot together one time. Then tap your left hand and your right foot together one time. Now start alternating this new pattern. If you can, try to go faster. What do you notice? The simultaneity breaks down *much* more quickly than in the first exercise. Furthermore, if you go too fast, you quickly revert to tapping the right hand with the right foot, and the left with the left.

We are hard-wired this way. The motor impulses for the right side of the body are originating from the left hemisphere of the brain, and vice-versa. When you try to cross the limbs over, you end up needing input from both sides of the brain at the same time.

This natural tendency is a phenomenon that drummers need to work to overcome as they learn to play more complicated patterns. And it's a great little exercise.

ON TECHNIQUE AND VARIANCES

One of the best videos on drumming technique is Jojo Mayer's *Secret Weapons of the Modern Drummer*. It's a three-hour treatise on all manner of stroke mechanics, complete with in-depth analysis of just about every way you can imagine hitting a drum. It's not for the casual enthusiast. To his credit, at the beginning of the video, Jojo explains that not every technique is for everyone, that each drummer should take away what he or she finds useful.

Most drummers learn technique from teachers or from videos and books. You can go study with different instructors or watch a handful of different videos and come away with some contradictory advice. I've had students come to me from other teachers and insist that there is only one way to do something. For example, some students parrot the common wisdom that playing the bass drum with the heel elevated off the pedal (heel up) gives a drummer more power and speed. While that may generally hold true, I know some drummers who can play just as loud and fast with their heel down. I once had a student who insisted that to play a good buzz roll, you had to slide your index finger out along the stick as it bounced. I never learned that technique, and disavowed him of that notion by demonstrating a very well-executed buzz roll using a totally different method.

Bubba Watson, the professional golfer and Masters champion, by most accounts has an ugly golf swing. It's about the loopiest golf swing on the PGA tour, and doesn't fit the mold of the perfect swing that most teachers try to get their students to emulate. Bubba is a self-taught golfer who has spent decades of his life playing golf. He's figured out a swing that works for him. I'm not saying that everyone can be like Bubba in creating their own oddball swing, or that the vast majority of amateur golfers wouldn't benefit from lessons with their local pro. There are always variances in technique that work differently for different people. Not every professional baseball hitter has the same swing or move to the ball. Not every PGA golfer has the same takeaway on their backswing. Not every great NBA 3-point shooter has the same release. They all figured out what works for them on an individual basis.

For every rule, there is an exception. Though I do have my own way of teaching stroke mechanics and hand technique, more than anything, I believe it's essential to learn to play in a way that doesn't create bad habits, which can lead to pain, or more frequently, to unnecessary limitations. Other than that, I'm a believer in doing whatever works for you.

THE COMFORT ZONE

When they sit down to play without any prompting, the majority of amateur drummers will play at the same tempo and volume almost every time. I call this the *Comfort Zone*. The more you play at a certain tempo and dynamic level, the more comfortable you become at them. The more natural they feel, the more you tend to practice at those same levels. Some students become so accustomed to their routine that when they play songs that are outside of that familiar range, they end up creeping up or down to where they're more habituated to playing.

For less experienced musicians, tempo and dynamics often go hand in hand. When they play faster they play louder, and when they play softer they slow down. They make the mistake of linking tempo and dynamics so that the two dimensions become dependent on one another, or at least influenced by each other.

To remedy this, I have students practice a wide range of speed and volume combinations: fast and soft (which can be very challenging), slow and loud, and at various levels in-between. Sometimes we use the metronome to force the tempo issue, sometimes not. Sometimes we'll use it just to reveal where the comfortable range is. It's important that they disassociate tempo and dynamics from each other. In doing so, they gain the ability to play comfortably at a wide range of settings and break out of their comfort zone.

VERSE 2

Drumming and Music

THE GROOVE IS ITS OWN REWARD

One of my favorite things to do with students is to spend an hour playing along with music. It's easy to get caught up reviewing technique and exercises, which I typically do with students week in and week out. Sometimes when I sense they need a break from the routine, or maybe they come in without having picked up their sticks all week, we'll shift gears and do something fun and outside of the box.

I tell them I'm going to cue up a bunch of different songs, most of which they won't know. I give them about 30 seconds to listen to each song, then ask them to start playing along—not to try to copy what they hear the drummer doing, but to come up with something they think sounds and feels good. I tell them to forget about the arrangement and not to worry about anticipating transitions—just to play what feels good to play.

This is one of the best ways I can help students learn to develop their instincts. I always try to frame my feedback in a positive way. I will also help them evaluate their approach and to think critically about what they are hearing and playing. I might suggest they listen a little more carefully to the bass or rhythm guitar to help determine how to phrase the bass drum part. Or I might ask them what they think the song is about, to describe the basic intent of the lyric content or the picture the artist is trying to paint, and to see if they can refine their part to reflect the character of the song.

I remind students to recognize the underlying rhythmic framework of each song: are the parts syncopated? Swinging? 16th note-based or strictly in 8th notes? Occasionally, there's an exception to the rule where the drum groove works well in rhythmic contrast to the bass and guitar parts, but for the most part, 8ths ask for 8ths, 16ths ask for 16ths, and triplets ask for triplet-based rhythms; straight goes with straight, swing goes with swing, and syncopated goes with syncopated. Paying careful attention to what you're hearing will always inform what you do.

Often when students are playing along with these songs, they'll throw in a lot of variations to their groove. Most of the time these variations will pull them out of the pocket—even when they don't create a timing issue, they will often distract from the flow of the song. If a student has been with me long enough, all is takes is a sideways glance from me and they respond with a knowing smile, as if to say, "Yeah, I know, I know." My goal is to get them to recognize these tendencies to overplay without my help, and to begin to develop their instincts for when songs can support variations and ornamentations in the groove and when they're better left alone.

With some encouragement, they end up simplifying what they started with. Sometimes, it may just take an adjustment to hi-hat tension, or the relative volume of the snare, or the punch of the kick. It can be surprisingly difficult, even on simple songs, to achieve just the right feeling. Usually with a little bit of shaping, there's a noticeable shift. Everything suddenly feels good, as if, with a slight adjustment to the dial, they were able to tune in a radio station more clearly.

When you are playing a part that is *in the groove*—musical and appropriate—there's no better feeling. Elusive as it may be, it's so important for drummers to know what this feels like. It's what great recordings and performances are made of.

PRACTICING TEMPOS: THE WISDOM OF BILL STEWART

I often read interviews with well-known drummers. The best ones have journalists asking really thoughtful and sometimes provocative questions instead of just fawning over a drummer and his or her accomplishments. As with people in general, you get some drummers who are really insightful and articulate, and others who are…less so. Once in a while I'll take away some nugget of advice that will stay with me for a long time. Some are so good that I pass them on to my students.

One such memorable piece of wisdom was from an interview with Bill Stewart, who's played with Maceo Parker, John Scofield, and Pat Metheny, among others, and is one of my favorite modern players. When the interviewer asked Bill what he practices, he answered, "Tempos." He explained that most of what he focuses on when he practices is being able to do what he already does comfortably at different tempos, honing his vast range of skills, coordination, patterns, styles, and creativity at a wide range of speeds.

To many drummers, that might not sound like much. Naturally, you need to acquire a vocabulary to get started, and there is no shortage of coordination exercises, drills and patterns to work on. But music is *flow*. And the vast majority of the time, that flow happens in steady time, or is at least supposed to. Bill understands that playing feels different at different speeds: what a drummer can play comfortably at one tempo, he cannot necessarily do as well at a faster, or even slower one. So he practices tempos.

Considering that most drummers need to work on their time more than anything else, he might be onto something.

TIME

Time as defined in music is the passage of regular temporal intervals, as indicated by the rhythms played by the various members of the band or ensemble, all referring to a common pulse as the basis for their rhythmic expressions. Time is also a *feeling*.

The goal of just about every band is to keep time together, with everyone's parts continuing to refer to the same commonly-felt pulse throughout the song. When one or more of the musicians accelerates or decelerates their implied pulse, the band begins to drift toward roughness, eventually coming unglued entirely if the disconnect becomes too extreme. Most often it happens more subtly, manifesting as a lack of tightness, a perception even the layperson can distinguish when listening to a live band; the music feels slightly rough or disjointed, like puzzle pieces forced together that don't fit perfectly.

In order for a band to stay in time together, each musician must constantly be listening to one another, to how their individual parts are fitting with the whole. As such, a band's time is established continuously over the course of playing a song, like rowers in a racing shell who need to match one another's cadence throughout a race. As soon as one person breaks rhythm, it affects the momentum and flow of the whole group.

I once had an adult student in one of my BandWorks classes who was a fairly competent player. He had a large vocabulary and could play complex parts and fills, but his time wasn't strong. The songs would invariably rush or drag, and, over the course of a minute or two, would fall apart because the drummer wasn't playing with the rest of the band. When I would point out that he was pushing or pulling the tempo, he would insist that his time was perfect. I had to pull out the metronome to prove it to him, though even then he still wouldn't fully accept his responsibility for it. He just wasn't listening to the rest of the band. I'd been guilty of it myself when I was younger. I would notice that a song would drag, but I would be so focused on my own playing, I would insist that I was steady while the song sagged. It doesn't usually work that way. If the entire song is rushing or dragging, it's almost always related to what's happening on the drums.

Even when musicians are listening attentively, the group time can be erratic: if one or more of the musicians (especially the drummer or bass player) is having difficulty executing their part in a controlled and consistent manner, the groove will have a herky-jerky feeling to it.

There is no better remedy for inconsistent time than practicing with a metronome. I tell my drum students to think of the metronome as a bass player playing quarter notes with perfect time. In order for them to stay locked in, they need to practice until they can execute their parts *with ease*. Only then can they begin to notice the very subtle fluctuations in their pacing, and start to hone their sense of steadiness.

When beginning drummers notice that they're not in sync with the metronome, they will often overcompensate to adjust. If they hear they're too slow, they speed up too much, overshooting their target tempo. Or vice versa. I teach them to make subtle shifts, gently leaning the groove forward or backward. I explain that great drummers live in that tiny space between the front edge and the back edge of the beat, and can hear it instantly when instrumental parts just barely begin to separate from each other—and make very minute, unnoticeably subtle adjustments to keep the band on track. I describe the difference between speeding up vs. rushing, and slowing down vs. dragging: you can play in time but still rush by playing too far in front of the beat, or drag by playing too far behind the beat (though most musicians use the terms "rushing" and "dragging" to mean speeding up and slowing down, respectively).

With my more advanced students, we'll practice playing on the front edge, back edge, and middle of the beat in relation to the metronome, and we'll listen to examples of music with drummers playing at various points in relation to the pulse.

It's a slow process. It takes time to work on your time.

* * *

The drummer lays down the rhythmic foundation for the band. His subdivisions of time establish a theoretical grid that continues throughout the song, upon which all other parts are juxtaposed. The next most important musician in establishing time is the bass player, who straddles the divide between rhythm and harmony. Since the bass player is usually responsible for playing the root of the chord at each chord change, she exerts great influence over the music by how she moves that note around in time. Of course, bass players also play arpeggios, walking lines, and rhythms with notes other than the root of the chord. Nonetheless, they are the arbiter of the harmonic context as the band moves from chord to chord. This filling up of the bottom end of the sonic spectrum makes the song feel whole, and the rhythm played by the bass goes a long way to defining both the pacing and energy of a song.

Thus, the bass and drums together lay the foundation of the groove and are the standard-bearers of the time-flow. It follows logically that much of the time, the drummer and the bass player need to focus closely on what one another is playing. My business partner with whom I started BandWorks, Steve Gibson, used to joke about the idea of the "three-legged bass." Like the three-legged race, where two people each tie one of their legs to one another and try to run in lock step, the bass player and the drummer should be similarly (if not literally) joined at the hip. It doesn't mean that the kick drum has to mirror the rhythms of the bass part note for note—it just means that they need to work seamlessly together, integrated to lay down the foundation of the groove.

Some of the most productive rehearsals I've ever had have been with just a bass player. By losing the rest of the rhythm section, we're able to strip down the grooves to their most essential elements, and really listen to how our parts fit together under close inspection. We might change how we attack the notes, adjust the duration or sustain of certain notes, and experiment with tone, dynamics, feel, and pocket. There's no better way to work on the groove. If the music in your band isn't sounding the way you'd like, the first place to listen is the bass and drums (vocalists notwithstanding). It's tough to build a good groove on a weak foundation.

* * *

Of course, classical music has frequently shifting tempos, mostly prescribed by the composer—but at some discretion of the conductor— to bring out the emotion in different passages of the music. Likewise, some modern jazz groups will deliberately pull and stretch the tempo to suit different sections of tunes. Even in some of the Motown and early rock/pop classics, there is a perceptible increase in tempo at the chorus. Elasticity of tempo is not by nature a bad thing. It's a very different thing to deliberately manipulate the time feel to make the music more expressive or nuanced, versus having the tempo of a song, particularly a groove-based song, move around unintentionally. Most of the time, that just makes the music lose its feel and groove.

* * *

The best musicians usually have the best time. When musicians have really good time, you can feel it right away. There is a consistency to their playing and clarity in their phrasing. It's comfortable and easy to play with them, and there is a quality that makes their music easy to listen to, as if the listener is unconsciously buoyed by the steadiness of the propulsion of the music. On the other hand, musicians with bad time are difficult to play with, and uncomfortable, even subconsciously, to listen to. Their music bends the listener's ear and requires more effort to listen to, like static on a radio channel; you can listen, but it's less pleasant and you have to concentrate to block out the white noise.

No matter what, you should not underestimate how important it is to have Good Time, nor how difficult it can be to play with a steady, locked in groove with your bandmates. If you want proof, try clapping in unison with another person. Listen carefully to how synchronized your claps are. Chances are great that you'll notice you don't clap at exactly the same time; you'll hear a slight flam on most of the claps. Now try adding another person, and another. You'll find that the more people you have attempting to clap in unison, the longer the clap lasts, from the beginning of the sound (the attack of the first clap) to the end (the decay of the last clap). More and more people start to clap just slightly ahead of the middle, and more start to lag behind. The same phenomenon will happen with larger groups of musicians. Even with trained timekeepers, the more people involved, the more difficult it is to keep the groove tight—which is one reason why larger ensembles will usually have a conductor to keep everybody referring to the same pulse (and of course, to indicate changes in dynamics, emotion, and tempo).

Over the past 27 years, I have watched hundreds of young drummers perform on stage. Of all the challenges aspiring young drummers face, the number one issue that comes up most frequently is *time*. Everyone needs to work on his time, including me. You're never done improving your timekeeping ability, and just because you may nail it one show doesn't mean your time will be perfect the next.

I have found it to be true that some people are born with better time than others. I have also generally found it to be true that female drummers have better time than male drummers. I don't know if that's universally true—it's just what I've seen in my experience as a teacher and concertgoer. In any case, with practice, you can improve your ability to maintain time more consistently: you can learn to hear a pulse, to count, to *feel* the beat, and to create rhythms with your body and your voice in time. After all, our bodies are sustained by the rhythmic pumping of our hearts. We are all drummers at the core.

TIME VS. TIMING

People often confuse time and timing. Time, as discussed, refers to the ability hold a steady tempo, or the execution of that ability. Timing refers to the spacing of notes and rhythmic phrases *in time*, corresponding to a regular rhythmic pulse. Timing certainly affects time, but I have seen some drummers who have pretty good time with some minor timing issues.

When drummers and other musicians have issues with timing, it's almost always due to an incorrect recognition of the space between the notes as opposed to the incorrect playing of the notes themselves. Often there's this little bit of anticipation or subtle anxiety about playing a riff that translates into a rushed fill or figure. When I hear students suffering from this affliction, I tell them not to focus on the notes, but on the space between them. Learn to hear and recognize the different timing gaps between the notes so that you know the sounds of silences as well as you know the sound of the notes.

Without silence, there is no music. It's kind of like looking at the negative space in a painting, like they teach you to do in art class. The more space there is between the notes, the more challenging it is to play them in time. So like my high school band director used to tell the percussion section all the time when we would disrupt band rehearsal with noodling: "Practice your rests!"

DYNAMICS

Playing without dynamics is like painting in monochrome. You can do it, and sometimes it can work, but for the most part it gets old fairly quickly. How long can you stare at a solid blue painting? The longer a song goes on without any dynamic contour, the less interesting it becomes. There's less to follow, less to tug on your ear. Newscasters know this. The next time you listen to the evening news on the radio or TV, pay attention to the cadence of the newscaster's voice. The good ones will almost "sing" the news, with a rise and fall in pitch and subtle changes in volume to emphasize different words, and to make it more compelling to listen to.

The same goes for music. Classical composers utilize this concept to great effect, and you can hear dynamics in every piece. The more expertly arranged and interpreted, the more expressive and evocative the piece. Jazz musicians know this too, and play with a great variety of inflection and articulation in order to improvise more expressively. And jazz solos will often have a dynamic arc to them, sometimes with several dynamic swells and falls. Dynamics mean change, and it's the changing that makes things interesting.

For the most part, dynamics have been lost in a lot of popular music today. There are still plenty of rock artists who recognize the importance of dynamics, and there are some exceptions in hip-hop and rap and modern pop, but I find that most of what's on the current hit list employs scant use of dynamics compositionally. It seems such a fundamental ingredient in music, it's a shame not to make use of it.

DYNAMICS VS. INTENSITY

One of the best shows I've seen was the South African jazz pianist Abdullah Ibrahim, playing with his trio at Yoshi's jazz club in Oakland, CA, in the smaller, more intimate venue, before they moved to Jack London Square. I don't think the band played louder than mezzo-piano (medium-soft) the entire night. It was one of the most intense performances I've ever witnessed.

The sweat was pouring off of Mr. Ibrahim's forehead, and he was rocking back and forth as he played. You could hear him grunting and moaning under his breath as he soloed. It seemed like he was pouring out his soul into every note. Musicians and audience alike were transported that night. I remember thinking afterward that it was one of the most intense shows I'd ever witnessed, and that volume is not the same thing as intensity.

TENSION AND RELEASE

If there is one concept that speaks to the essence of how we experience music, it is *tension and release*. This is also the mechanism that keeps us procreating as a race. It's no surprise, then, that the terms "jazz" and "rock & roll" both evolved as euphemisms for sex. Different branches, same roots.

Tension in music can be created in any of three fundamental

ways: melodically, harmonically, and rhythmically. Often they will go together and complement one another, but other times you can have one or two elements without the other(s). You can also create tension dynamically. Dynamics is like a separate channel that can cut across all three of the others and change their effects, respectively.

Music theory goes a long way toward explaining western harmony and why certain chords sound the way they do, with different degrees of tension and color built into them, depending on their extensions and voicings. It also examines the way these chords sound in relation to one another and how notes sound in chordal context (i.e., melody in the context of harmony). Sometimes overlooked is the rhythmic element, how changing the rhythm or pacing of a piece can have an impact on the listener.

Often, drummers will apply syncopation to underscore other tension happening in the music, heightening the effect of the harmonic or melodic tension and subsequent release. It could be a melody about to climax, a resolving chord change, or even something as simple as marking the end of a four-bar phrase. They'll do this with any of a wide range of tools, from the subtle addition of one note in the bass drum part to a highly syncopated fill. You can hear it (barely) in Al Jackson's very subtle bass drum variation (he moves it from a downbeat-based pattern to all the upbeats) on the last bar of the chorus in Otis Redding's "(Sitting on the) Dock of the Bay." And you can hear it as a signature fill fraught with tension in Phil Collins' "In the Air Tonight," so recognizable that people will air drum along with it.

All good composers know how to use different modalities of tension and release to evoke a feeling, with the notes, chords, rhythm, and dynamics working together to create a visceral effect. As you start to notice the moments or passages full of tension and release in music, it'll make you more aware of composition and structure. But even if you don't notice them consciously, you can't help but feel good when you hear them.

DEGREE OF SWING *(for Steve)*

When I was a teenager, my band director explained to me the difference between straight 8th notes and swung 8th notes. From that simple distinction, I assumed all music that had a swinging feeling was based in a triplet feel, with the middle note of each triplet omitted; there was straight music and there was triplet-based swung music, and that was it.

Not so.

In many styles of music, you will find songs with different *degrees* of swing. For the purposes of this discussion, let's define as "swinging" any groove that is not straight. If the upbeats (or the second and fourth 16th notes of each beat, if it's a 16th note-based groove) move even the slightest fraction later than normal, the music will have a looser feel, leaning toward swinging. How far those notes move can vary from style to style and song to song.

There are some general qualities of swing that can be discerned in different genres of music from different places. Chicago blues tends to have a very triplet-based pocket. A lot of New Orleans funk tends to have a straighter-than-triplet swing pocket. (In New Orleans they refer to the in-between swing and straight feel so common there as "playing between the cracks.") Texas blues tends to swing to a greater degree, with a wider gap between each downbeat and the following upbeat. Brazilian samba has a different feel entirely, with the middle two 16th note subdivisions of each beat swung, and the first and fourth more straight. (My head hurt the first time I tried to wrap my brain around that.) There are always exceptions to the general rule. I've heard Chicago blues bands play some straight-leaning shuffles, and bands from New Orleans play a very swung 8th note groove.

Since the early 2000s, some hip-hop and neo-soul bands have been exploring the idea of a deliberately inconsistent swing feel. Their drummers play with the pocket by moving the swing feeling back and forth over the course of a song, playing behind the beat and then on top of it. ("Slim and Juicy" by Chris Dave and the Drumhedz is a good example of this; the concept was first introduced by hip-hop producer J Dilla, and subsequently refined by The Roots' drummer Ahmir Questlove.) It makes sense that musicians would explore breaking down the *a priori* assumption of smooth time-flow. Many of the most groundbreaking musicians and bands deconstructed some hitherto unexamined assumptions about music and the way it was supposed to sound—whether it be in the context of harmony (Thelonious Monk), rhythm (James Brown), or melody (Joni Mitchell). At some point, artists will rebel against every convention and preconceived notion that boxes them in.

I like to demonstrate the concept of "swing degree" for my students with a visual aid by lining up four evenly spaced drum sticks on the floor like so:

I	I	I	I
(1)	(e)	(&)	(a)

I suggest that each stick represents a 16th note subdivision of one beat ("1-e-&-a," in common Western music nomenclature). I'll usually put colored sticks on the "1" and the "&" counts to differentiate them more clearly. This spacing of notes, which in theory continues on through the entirety of a song, is what we call "straight." The subdivisions are evenly separated, and the rhythms have an even feel to them.

Then I'll roll the second and fourth sticks over to the right, like so:

$$
\begin{array}{cccc}
\text{I} & \text{I} \quad \text{I} & & \text{I} \\
(1) & (e) \ (\&) & & (a)
\end{array}
$$

Now the "e" and the "a" counts, referred to as the 16th note subdivisions, are later than halfway between their respective 8th note subdivisions (the "1" and the "&"). The resulting rhythm has a lilting feeling, like a heartbeat. The "e" and the "a" counts are moved later the exact same degree, and this delay needs to be maintained consistently throughout the song in order for it to groove and stay in the pocket.

You can play with the degree of delay. You can move the "e" and "a" just a little to the right:

$$
\begin{array}{cccc}
\text{I} & \text{I} & \text{I} & \text{I} \\
(1) & (e) & (\&) & (a)
\end{array}
$$

Thus giving the song just a slight hint of swing, or looseness, as compared with a straight feel.

You can also swing to the extreme, where the notes are practically on top of one another:

$$
\begin{array}{ccc}
\text{I} & \text{I} \ \text{I} & \text{I} \\
(1) & (e)(\&) & (a)
\end{array}
$$

Sometimes the degree of swing will be quantized, which is to say based on a whole number or round percentage; you can swing the 16ths like they're based in 16th note triplets, or as dotted 16ths with 32nds, for example. Those are just two points on the spectrum. And regardless of whether the swing fits into a countable, quantized subdivision, the degree of swing needs to be *felt*.

I like to use the funk classic "Pass the Peas" by the J.B.'s (James Brown's band from 1970 through the early '80s) to demonstrate this concept aurally. I have four versions of this tune in my library, though there are more versions that have been recorded. The versions I have are:

The J.B.'s (from *Pass the Peas: The Best of the J.B.'s*)
Maceo Parker (from *Life on Planet Groove*)
The Legendary Meters & the J.B. Horns
  (from *Funky Good Time*)
The J.B.'s (from *James Brown's Funky People*)

Each rendition of this song has a different pocket. I play these back to back and tap out the 16th notes to demonstrate the differing degrees of swing in each version. The *Funky People* version is decidedly straighter than the others. The Maceo groove is the swingiest. The other two are somewhere in-between.

Of course, the same concept applies to 8th note-based grooves, like rock songs and shuffles. You can hear this on different versions of the blues classic "Kansas City," from the loping triplet, almost country version by Wilbert Harrison to the harder swung version by Albert King. Similarly, Bonnie Raitt swings her version of "Thing Called Love," while John Hiatt recorded his with an in-between feel, not quite straight with just a little hint of swing (a great example of a "between the cracks" kind of groove).

Most students typically have a more difficult time playing music with a swung feel than straight. My guess is it's because of the music they've listened to. Pop and rock music are usually played straight, whereas most funk, soul, hip-hop, and reggae have a swinging feel. I also think that music that swings requires a greater degree of skill to execute and is more challenging to control and perform consistently.

Most jazz music is based in triplets, and therefore swung.

But even in a jazz context, drummers can play the basic cymbal pattern (the main propulsive element of the swing feel) with varying degrees of swing. Degree of swing can also be determined by tempo. At slower speeds, with more space between the notes, there is more room to delay the notes, which are more easily perceivable as distinct. The faster the tempo, the less room there is to swing the notes, as the beats are closer together, until at a certain speed, there is no discernible difference between straight and swung. The music is so fast that it becomes almost impossible to swing the upbeats anymore (nor would it sound good if you did), and the 8th notes are played evenly.

Without a definitive mathematical marker to determine the degree of swing, it must be created anew each and every time a band plays a song. With practice and experience, drummers and other musicians become adept at replicating the feel of a given pocket at a given tempo. Like so many other aspects of playing music, it is a skill that can be learned and honed. After all, we are all swinging: the heart doesn't beat two thumps spaced evenly in time—they come in closer pairs, with a longer gap between the second of the two heartbeats and the first of the next pair. From even before our first breaths, we are all, majestically, perfectly, swinging in time.

ON RUDIMENTS

Drumming rudiments are patterns played by the hands with sticks. You can certainly apply them to the feet or add foot patterns to be played underneath them, but they were originally conceived to be played with the hands. They consist of a number of sticking patterns (e.g., a *paradiddle*, one of the most fundamental rudiments, is simply a pattern of playing RLRR LRLL); *flam* rudiments, wherein a drummer plays two strokes (R-L or L-R) almost but not quite simultaneously, thereby emphasizing the note and making it sound fatter; *drag* rudiments, where the drummer plays a double-bounce grace note before a stroke or pattern; and various drum rolls. There are hundreds of variations on the rudiments, as you can create permutations of them by varying the sticking, accents, or ornamentations in each pattern.

Individually, the rudiments don't really sound like much. They're like coordination puzzles for your hands. In aggregate, they cover a very wide range of sonic and rhythmic possibilities. Just as actors practice tongue twisters to become comfortable with various syllabic combinations and patterns, drummers practice rudiments to familiarize themselves with a wide range of techniques and patterns that ultimately formed the basis of modern drumming.

The earliest history of drumming rudiments comes from Swiss mercenaries in the 15th century, who began to use the side drum (which would later become known as the snare drum) to play rhythmic sequences using sticks in both hands in order to signal and orchestrate military maneuvers.[1] These sequences, which increased in complexity over time, required learning a series of foundational patterns that became known as *rudiments*. Over a couple of centuries, the playing of these drumming patterns migrated through France, England, and Scotland (where the practice laid the foundation for what would become the Highland pipe and drum bands), and, eventually, to the American colonies in the 18th century. As the practice of playing rudiments moved from country to country, each local cadre of drummers would add their own twists, adapting and modifying them, though none so much as those in America.[2]

By the 19th century, there were already a number of published volumes of rudimental exercises in the United States. To clear up the inevitable confusion coming from so many disparate sources, a group of drummers in the 1930s, including William F. Ludwig (namesake of the famous Ludwig Drum Company), created the National Association of Rudimental Drummers (NARD).

1 Matt Dean, The Drum: A History (Scarecrow Press, 2012)
2 ibid

They decided to distill the existing drumming rudiments culled from various sources into the 13 core rudiments, to which they added an additional 13, comprising a list of what are now known as the 26 "official" rudiments. The decision regarding which 13 rudiments to add was based on a survey NARD sent to its approximately 250 registered members. (In retrospect, this seems like a pretty arbitrary way to codify something so fundamental. It's possible the arbiters of these 26 rudiments didn't know at the time how influential their work would be.) In 1985, the Percussive Arts Society decided to add another 14 rudiments, bringing the total number of official rudiments to 40, though there are factions of the drumming community that still only recognize the original 26.

For a number of years when I was first teaching lessons, I didn't focus very much on rudiments. I'd cover the basic ones (paradiddles, flam taps, etc.), but didn't put my students through too many paces with them. I've since changed my approach, and spend more time on rudiments than I used to. For my advanced students, I'll have them work through the Wilcoxon books (particularly *Modern Rudimental Swing Solos for the Advanced Drummer*), which, in every single case has totally transformed their hands and, subsequently, their overall playing.

Some teachers swear by the rudiments. I know of one well-known college percussion professor who opined that, "If your teacher isn't teaching you rudiments, you should find a new teacher." I don't subscribe to that belief. I do think the rudiments are important to learn, if for no other reason than that they give a drummer an immensely useful vocabulary, and a basis on which to build technique. They are not the be-all-end-all, unless you play in a marching band or drum corps, which is essentially all rudiments all the time for the snare drummers.

* * *

The drum set as we recognize it today debuted around the late 1910s. The first commercially available modern drum kit, made by the Ludwig Drum Company, was released in 1918. There were certainly modern snare drums and other percussion instruments around well before that, but it was the collection of these various instruments and contraptions (hence the name "trap set") into one array that was the genesis of the instrument as we know it today. Most significantly, the invention of the bass drum pedal, and subsequently the low-boy, or sock cymbal (the precursor to the hi-hat)* freed up the drummer to play patterns with the feet at the same time as the hands, thus enabling multiple layers of coordinated rhythms to be performed simultaneously.

The instruments left over from the civil war military bands became the instruments of the early jazz bands, and it was the rudimental snare drummers who naturally became the first drum set players. The early jazz greats Buddy Rich, Sid Catlett, Gene Krupa, and Chick Webb were all masters of the rudiments, as were the generation who followed them, and the generation after that. While it's true that rudiments fell out of favor to some extent with the advent of rock music, there are still many rock and pop drummers who are steeped in the rudiments and use them prominently in their playing. In truth, all drummers utilize at least some rudiments in their playing whether they realize it or not. Even the simple single-stroke roll, alternating sticks R-L-R-L, is a rudiment—and every drummer uses that move extensively, among a number of other very common patterns.

---

*Initially the hi-hat cymbals were perched on a pedal just above the floor, until someone had the great idea to raise them up on a pole so drummers could hit them with sticks in addition to being able to close them together with the foot.

WHY IT'S IMPORTANT FOR DRUMMERS
TO KNOW THE MELODY

In pop and rock songs, it's important to be familiar with the lyrics so you can know what the song is about and what emotion the song is trying to deliver. It's helpful to know the melody too, so you can follow it and support it in your playing as appropriate. In jazz, it is vital. When I was younger and less experienced, I would often find myself playing jazz tunes on gigs that I had never heard before. While it is possible to keep time and know the form of a tune, there is a huge difference between playing a tune you know and playing one you don't.

To begin with, the melody of a jazz tune is the only part of the song that is predictable. It's the part that people recognize as *the song*, and it's the drummer's job to punctuate it musically. If you don't know it, your punctuation will likely sound more random and less relevant. If you do know the song and have developed even a basic jazz vocabulary (some degree of left-hand independence, to start with), you can play the song like you know it and get *inside* it. It's the difference between playing *along with* the tune and having your playing be a *part of* the tune.

SOLOING

One of the most challenging things for me to teach is how to solo. Most other jazz instruments usually focus on harmony, chord theory, and scales as the basis for improvisation. Since drums are not a pitched instrument (though some drummers do tune their toms to pitches), we focus on entirely different elements in exploring how to fill up space.

I tell my students to think like a horn player when they solo. Clean phrasing is one of the most important elements of a good solo. Without it, your ideas become a mish-mash of unintelligible and out of time gibberish. Horn players, only able to play one note at a time, must think and play in discreet phrases, even if those phrases link together or have many notes in them. "Play so that if someone were listening, at any moment, they could repeat the last phrase you played," I recommend.

One of the best pieces of advice I ever heard was to practice "singing," or vocalizing, your solo. When you speak or sing, you tend to do so in clear and distinct phrases, and it can even lend a melodic quality to your improvising. If you can play what you say, your playing will tend to be cleaner and easier to understand.

I like to start students out by asking them to practice a four-bar improvised solo, keeping it simple and easy. Trading fours (alternating four bars of time with four bars of solo) is the first step toward constructing longer ideas that can hold together and begin to establish some kind of arc. If drummers have trouble with trading fours, I ask them to just play a one-bar fill, then link two of them together, then four. Once a drummer can competently stay in time and play the correct number of bars while trading fours, we work on 8's, then 12's. Then I have them practice soloing over a 12-bar blues form, and then a 32-bar AABA form.

While there are some circumstances where a drummer will solo over an open vamp, most commonly (in jazz, at least) solos will be over a set form, the same form that the other instrumentalists have been soloing over. Learning to be aware of where you are in the form is critical to playing good, musical solos.

When I was in college, I would go down to the jazz jam sessions at the local jazz club in Ann Arbor on Sunday nights (the Bird of Paradise) and wait for my turn to sit in. When it came time for me to play solos, I had a lot of good rhythmic ideas. I just couldn't keep track of where I was in the form. Within 12 bars, I'd be lost, soloing in time and tracking the downbeat, but not knowing where I was in the tune. After a minute or so, the musicians would realize that I was lost and someone would count the band back in to the head, while I turned red in the face and avoided eye contact.

There are two effective ways to learn to keep track of the form while you solo. The first is what I call the *math approach*: if you can learn to instinctively feel four-bar phrases while you improvise (which in itself is predicated upon good phrasing), you can easily track how many four-bar phrases you play. If you're playing a 12-bar blues, you know they come in batches of three four-bar phrases, and you can start to count them as 12-bar units. Or, if it's an AABA form, you can count four eight-bar phrases and know you've completed a chorus. It's easy enough to learn to solo in four-bar phrases, and you can keep them going ad infinitum. I'm not a big fan of the math approach. Though your improvisation will add up correctly and you can know where you are in the form, this approach can sometimes lead to clunky and unimaginative soloing, often without any kind of dynamic arc to the overall solo.

I much prefer a melodic approach. Some of the best jazz drummers will play the melody when they solo—not literally, but interpretively. You can hear the melody as the source of their inspiration as they embellish, augment, color, and play with tension and release. They reinvent their own version of the melody through rhythmic devices like repetition and theme and variation. If you listen carefully, you can often hear the melody in the solo.

Of course, to solo from a melodic standpoint requires that you *know the melody by heart*. Which is another reason I teach my students to learn to sing the melody of the tunes they play. Then, when they sing their solo, you can hear the melody in their rhythmic and tonal interpretation.

The only way to really learn to solo effectively is to practice it. You can listen to the greats for inspiration, but you have to take the plunge into the abyss over and over to gain the confidence to navigate through it.

I vividly remember the very first drum solo I ever took. It was in high school during a jazz combo rehearsal. We were playing

"Lester Leaps In" (originally recorded by the Count Basie Orchestra), and after the sax solo, my friend, who was the combo leader and most experienced jazz player, shouted, "Drum solo!" Everybody stopped playing except me. I had no idea what to do. "What do you mean, drum solo?!" I said, in shock. "Just keep playing!" he implored. So I just kept playing time, adding some punctuations here and there. It wasn't much of a drum solo, except that it was the drums playing without accompaniment, and therefore a solo. But it was a start!

I like to encourage my students to take risks, especially when it comes to improvising. Sometimes we can spend an entire lesson just working on a 12-bar solo, experimenting with different dimensions and approaches. There are so many elements that you can play with and contrast: dynamics, busyness vs. sparseness, color, using only certain parts of the kit, keeping time with the hi-hat or not, playing a "time" solo, etcetera. They may play an entire solo on ride and snare only...or toms only...or rims only...or only playing one note per bar...or playing constant triplets the whole way through, with different triplet sticking patterns. There are so many ways to experiment and to learn to apply the tools in your toolbox. It's an adventure, and you really can get better at it very quickly if you work at it.

I'll have my more advanced students transcribe solos from some famous recordings and learn to play them. This is a great way to pick up licks and ideas from some of the great jazz players. We all beg and borrow, and there's no shame in that. If you listen to any drummer long enough (or any instrumentalist, for that matter), you'll hear the same ideas pop up often. And while it's good to have a nice bag of tricks, you want your playing, and especially your soloing, to sound fresh and relevant to the moment.

TRANSCRIBING

In the process of transcribing over a thousand drum charts, I've learned a lot about what makes a good drum part. Close listening to so many recordings has informed my own aesthetic. It's taught me taste and restraint and has deepened my appreciation and understanding of *pocket* and *dynamics*. I highly recommend that any aspiring drummer learn how to transcribe. In addition to developing your ear, you'll learn so much about groove structure and phrasing and get to dig different drummers' musical concepts. Plus, you'll be able to borrow all sorts of great ideas and licks.

The first time I ever transcribed anything was an assignment for a college improvisation class. We were asked to pick a song and transcribe the part for our instrument. I ended up choosing Dave Brubeck's "Blue Rondo a la Turk" off of the iconic *Time Out* album, with the great Joe Morello on drums. The song is in 9/8, but the drum part is very clear and at the time I was very interested in odd time compositions. I dug how the song played with the phrasing of the bar and how Joe's parts were orchestrated to fit it. I was struck by how he had come up with such perfectly musical parts to play out of just his imagination and instincts.

Delving into that tune inspired me to transcribe other songs, so I started to do it as an enjoyable project for myself outside of the requirements of my class. I chose mostly songs I liked, sometimes transcribing just a a few bars or a part that interested me.

It wasn't until I started BandWorks with my friend Steve Gibson in 1993 that I began to transcribe prolifically. For each rock band workshop, we selected five songs to rehearse for an eight-week session. I transcribed the drum parts for the songs, figuring it would help drummers learn the songs more easily. Usually I'd write out the first pass through the verse and chorus, then the bridge and any other meaningfully different parts. Occasionally, I'd write out an entire song note-for-note, especially if the drummer played a more dynamic part that kept changing throughout the song.

I end up transcribing something just about every day for one of my students during lessons. Since it can be time consuming, I try to limit it to just a few minutes out of the lesson. Anything requiring more time, I'll work on at home. As my students progress, I try to teach them to transcribe on their own, and we'll often make an ongoing project out of writing out a song or drum solo. Usually, the most challenging part for them is parsing out the different parts of the drum kit. I'll have them adjust the EQ on their laptop or device to try to highlight the different frequencies and hear the parts of the kit more distinctly (bass on the bottom, cymbals on top, snare and toms in the mid-range). We'll use it as a listening exercise, and I'll lead them to answers one baby step at a time (Can you hear the snare drum on two and four? Any other places? Do you notice the ghost note?), until they can start to manage on their own. When they bring in transcriptions they've worked on, we'll listen together and review it for errors or omissions and work on articulation and dynamics.

More than anything, I've learned a lot about *what not to play* from transcribing. Most popular music on the radio turns out to have fairly straightforward drum parts. Which makes sense. Simple parts are easier to listen to, easier to digest. They don't require as much attentive listening, and they support easy melodies and simple harmonic progressions (this is not a value judgment, as there's plenty of pop music I enjoy). It's kind of ironic, because as drummers we spend so many years learning all manner of complicated coordination patterns and techniques, but in the end, many successful drummers of pop and rock bands hardly tap into what they are capable of playing. Buddy Rich famously said, "If you don't have ability, you end up playing in a rock band." But there is great subtlety involved in playing just the right musical part within the limitations of a pop or rock song. (So no, I don't agree at all with Buddy Rich.)

I've also learned that charts can't tell the whole story. You can get the mechanics down on paper, and you can try to indicate expression with accents, half-open hi-hats, ghost notes, and articulation marks. But there's just no way you can account in notation for the color, energy, feel, groove, swing, and expressiveness of a human playing the drums. I've had students play parts off of a chart note-for-note and sound nothing like the original recording, whereas other students can play something very different from the chart and sound much more musical.

Transcribing is an effective tool for copying what good drummers have played, for picking up tricks and licks, and for developing your instincts by modeling good players' ideas and concepts. But charts will never get you all the way there, and in some cases can even impede your progress toward sounding good. If you're too focused on reading the page, you're not going to be listening as attentively. And if you're adhering to a pre-fab paint-by-numbers kind of approach to playing, you're not bringing your creativity and musicality to bear on the music.

THE IMPORTANCE OF UNDERSTANDING SONG FORM

I once got a call for a gig that was happening that same night. The bass player in the band was a friend of mine and recommended me when their drummer had to bail at the last minute for personal reasons. I didn't know the band or their music. They were playing primarily original songs written by the singer/songwriter, mostly in a country/roots rock style, in addition to a few familiar covers. Seeing as it was at a local bar, it wasn't a super high-stakes gig. Thankfully, the patrons would be more interested in drinking beer and playing pool than listening attentively to the music. Nevertheless, I wanted as always to put my best foot forward, especially when playing with musicians I didn't know. I still had a full day ahead teaching lessons, and there was no way I was going to be able to learn any new music before the gig. I explained as much to the bandleader. He assured me that was okay, and that he knew I'd do my best. He was just desperate to have a drummer show up for the gig. I told him I'd see him at 7 pm.

When I arrived to set up, I encouraged the bass player to be especially demonstrative with visual cues. I asked him to whisper to me the time signature, the style, and the general vibe before each song we were about to play. "Chicago shuffle in 4," he'd say, or, "Country ballad," or, "Think 'Beast of Burden' by the Stones." I watched him for cues, and I paid close attention to the singer's body language. When I saw him take a deep breath and lift his guitar ever so slightly, I knew we were headed for the chorus. Endings were of course a challenge, but many of the songs had predictable rock 'n' roll and blues endings (think "Johnny B. Goode," etc.). I didn't catch them all, but I got most of them.

After the gig, the bandleader came up to me. "Holy shit," he said in disbelief. "How did you do that?! It's like you've already been playing in my band for a couple of months!" I was flattered. "Thanks!" I said, happy for the recognition. I had felt pretty good about it. Since I had played with the bass player before and we had a good rapport, the songs grooved nicely. I was careful to pay attention to dynamics, and listened hard as we played so that whatever I didn't know before the first verse, I knew by the second. Rather than seeing it as a scary thing, I decided to treat it like a fun challenge. Without expecting to nail everything, I chose to enjoy trying to get as much as I could. I was on my toes the entire night, super focused. It was like walking a tightrope, knowing that falling would be ok. The next day the bandleader called to ask if I would replace their current drummer, who was on his way out. I ended up playing with the band for about four years.

More than anything, I attribute my success that night to my recognition and understanding of song form. Almost all of the songs followed fairly predictable familiar structures. (If it were a prog-rock band, I am sure I would not have fared so well!) I was able to maintain awareness of where I was, and most of the time, accurately forecast where we were going. I would take risks playing fills and adding lifts when I thought we were heading to a chorus, and break it down when I knew we were hitting the verse after the solo. I'd mix it up on the bridge. And I'd often start with a stripped down part for the intro, unless the bass player told me to hit it hard from the start. In all honesty, the playing was the easy part. Learning the arrangements on the fly was the real challenge.

* * *

As an instructor at BandWorks, I've worked with many dozens of developing musicians who are trying to learn five or six songs in the course of eight weeks. While that may not seem like too difficult a task for some, with only eight two-hour rehearsals, there is little time to waste in learning to play each tune with the appropriate groove, feel, and character, and making sure all the parts line up where they should. Similarly, I've worked with many private students who are playing in gigging bands or preparing for auditions and need to learn a large number of songs in a short amount of time.

Just about every professional drummer has been faced with the challenging (but fun!) scenario where we need to learn a gig's worth of songs very quickly. In my experience, the two most important requirements to learning new songs efficiently are:

- Recognizing the song form
- Playing with the proper feel, or character. (I'll tackle this concept in a separate essay.)

I can't tell you how many times I've witnessed rehearsals with amateur musicians stall or grind to a halt because someone didn't know what was supposed to happen next. Bands waste so much time and can experience so much frustration when musicians don't know the form. Even with songs that are familiar, musicians often won't have a full grasp of the song structure. I've seen some drummers, for example, play all the way through a song perfectly on one try, only to make arrangement mistakes on subsequent efforts. Or they rely on other band members to know the road map, catching hits, groove changes, and dynamic shifts a couple of beats late.

There's no need to leave your playing up to chance. Being familiar with the song form on every song you play will save you time and embarrassment, and make it appear that you know the songs well, even if some of the details may be missing.

Think of knowing the form like knowing the driving directions to some familiar destination, like school or work. If you ride as a passenger in the car each day, you might know the general way to get from here to there, and you may recognize some familiar landmarks along the way. You can get to your destination without really paying attention, since someone else knows the precise route. But as soon as you're in the driver's seat, you realize that unless you know how to get all the way from A to B on your own, there's a good chance you're going to get lost.

On the other hand, once you know the way through a song like the back of your hand, you can get there almost without even thinking about it. You can know who made the mistake where, and what was supposed to happen when. Better still, you can lead the band along the way, putting in fills or visual cues at the proper times to set up transitions, helping your bandmates with a turn signal or two.

Even if you don't know the groove or haven't come up with a part, having a sense of when to make changes to support the composition will help you define your parts and can really bring out the contrast and dynamics of the song. If you have a drum chart or can look over a chord chart or lead sheet, the form is usually indicated for you. But if you don't have the luxury of charts or can't read, you're left with your ears to figure it out. (And even if you can read it, it's different from knowing the form by heart.) Like so much else regarding playing music, it comes down to listening.

The vast majority of rock and pop songs use the same structural building blocks and arrange them in some (usually) predictable order. Once you become familiar with these common elements and sequences, you'll be able to recognize the form of a tune and know how it goes after only one or two times listening through it. Furthermore, you'll become so familiar with a handful of conventional arrangement progressions that you'll often be able to reliably predict what happens next in a song—even if you've never heard it before! Naturally there are many exceptions, but you'll be surprised how good at guessing you can become.

The basic elements of the rock/pop song form are:

Intro
The intro of the song may be played by any number of instruments, from one instrument to the entire band. Sometimes the intro will be subdivided into a number of parts (e.g. the piano plays the first 4 bars, then bass enters for 4, then drums for 8 more). Usually the intro lasts until the first verse begins. On rare occasions, a chorus will precede a verse.

Verse
This is the part with the singing. Songs usually have different lyrics for each verse, though sometimes, especially in Blues, verses can be repeated. Typical length: 8, 12, or 16 bars.

Pre-chorus
The pre-chorus is much less common than the chorus, but many songs have one. It sounds very different from the verse, and will usually have the same words each time, distinguishing it from the verse. The pre-chorus usually sets up the chorus in a very obvious way. Depending on the song, the pre-chorus might be considered part of the verse. Typical length: 8 bars.

Chorus

When you hit the chorus, you'll know it. It's usually fuller sounding, often louder than the verse or pre-chorus, and has the same words every time. It's the hook, the refrain, the part that makes you smile and want to sing along. Often it adds harmony vocals and heavier guitars. The drummer will often go to the ride cymbal. It's the payoff from the verse, the release, the catchy part of the song that everybody knows. Typical length: 8, 12, or 16 bars. Sometimes there will be an additional 4 or 8 bars of verse groove, which can act as a link to set up the following verse.

Bridge (or Interlude, or Middle 8)

The Bridge is an often-misunderstood section, mainly because it sounds like neither the verse nor the chorus. Often it will change key (modulate), or have a distinct feeling from the verse and chorus. Typically there will be some kind of feel change that accompanies the bridge, though not always. The bridge isn't usually very long, as it acts to bridge the chorus back to the verse or a solo, and offer a break from the monotony of the verse/chorus progression. Typical length: 8 bars, sometimes longer.

Vamp

A vamp is a repeating section of a song, usually 1, 2, or 4 bars long, which repeats over and over some set number of times or until some cue. Solos will often be played over a vamp. A vamp is usually of undetermined length, to be ended by spontaneous decision of the soloist or bandleader. When bands jam or rock out, it's usually over a vamp, or a repeated chorus, which can also function as a vamp.

Solos

Not every song has a solo. When they are played, they can be as short as 4 bars, or as long as 10 minutes or more. Solos can be played over the verse form, chorus, bridge, vamp, or any combination of sections. Most often solos will be over either a verse, chorus, verse/chorus, or a vamp. The vamps can be either a set length or open-ended until cue.

Outro or Coda

The outro or coda (ending) of a song can take many different forms. Some songs will fade out over a chorus vamp. Or they may revert to the intro. Other times the band will play a set number of bars or repeat the turnaround until hitting some rhythmic figure together.

Songs may have any combination of the above elements, or omit some of them entirely. Some songs may have only a verse and chorus. Others, like a standard blues, will have a 12-bar form that repeats over and over, whether there are verses or solos. Still others may have additional sections, where there is an elongated or shortened verse or chorus, a double chorus, or a different section entirely that doesn't really fit into any of the above categories (though this is less common).

There are no absolutes regarding form, since the possibilities are limitless, after all. But the vast majority of rock and pop songs are structured according to very common blueprints, using the same handful of building blocks. Once you can recognize these basic form elements very quickly, you'll be amazed at how much more efficiently you'll be able to learn new songs.

PROPULSION

I like the word *propulsion*—it encapsulates the drummer's job in the vast majority of musical situations. A drummer can even play behind the beat, but still propel the music forward. He can rev at whatever speed is required, even at a snail's pace, or at a whisper volume. The drummer is almost always the engine that drives the music forward.

WHY THERE ARE MORE GOOD DRUMMERS
NOW THAN EVER BEFORE

People ask me all the time if I think there are more good drummers in the world now than there used to be 40 or 50 years ago. I don't know how you could possibly make a case that there aren't. For starters, there are about three billion more people on the planet now, which means there are a lot more drummers. Remo, the world's largest drumhead manufacturing company, estimates that 1% of the world's population are drummers. My guess is it's actually higher. But more than population growth, I think the most significant reason for the explosion of the number of drummers is that there are so many more resources available to young drummers now than there ever used to be. It's also worth noting that every country in the world has had some sort of drum as an indigenous musical instrument.

Up until the 1970s, there weren't that many instructional books around. There was *Stick Control*, the Wilcoxon books, Jim Chapin's seminal *Advanced Techniques for the Modern Drummer*, Ted Reed's *Syncopation*, and a couple of dozen others, but the primary way drummers learned was by listening to records and playing along (still an effective and important thing to do!). If you were lucky, great drummers like Philly Joe Jones and Art Blakey would come through your city, and if you were really fortunate, you might be able to hang with them and ask for a lesson while they were in town. Of course there were teachers, and some notably great ones—Billy Gladstone and Sanford Moeller, then later Alan Dawson and Jim Chapin, among others—but in general the resources were few and difficult to find compared with what for today's drummer is just a few clicks away.

With the advent of the Internet came widely accessible music from all over the world. Instead of having to go to the record store to see if they had the latest Clifford Brown album or waiting until

Max Roach came to town, you can now listen to every recording that band ever made from the comfort of your home, and for just a few dollars! Today there are hundreds of very excellent instructional books and a myriad of videos on just about any drumming topic widely available for free on YouTube. Granted, with the voluminous amount of content, a good deal of it isn't very well presented, or accurate. However, if you look around, you can find excellent quality videos and teaching resources on just about any topic under the sun.

I want to make an important distinction between good technical drummers and good musical drummers. While there are many more very skilled drummers around today, that doesn't necessarily mean that there are more *musical* players than there used to be. Sometimes they are the same, but often they are not. One of my favorite quotes from Tony Williams, the jazz drumming titan who started playing with Miles Davis when he was 17, is: "Playing fast around the drums is one thing. To play music, to play with people for others to listen to, that's something else. That's a whole other world." Though there are thousands of really great technicians in the world, there are a much smaller number of good, musical drummers. Access to resources alone doesn't make someone better able to groove, play with good feel, or play inspired music.

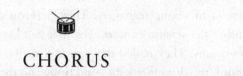

CHORUS

The Artistry of Drumming

OWNING WHAT YOU PLAY

If you feel apologetic or unsure about what you're playing, you're going to sound apologetic or unsure. Believing in what you play is one of the most important requirements to sounding good. I've watched and heard so many drummers play good parts without any conviction. No matter what you play, it doesn't sound good unless you take *ownership* of it. Conversely, I've also heard some drummers who didn't have a whole lot of vocabulary or skill really lay in to their playing and sound great.

There was a time when I was teaching two different BandWorks classes of young teenagers. They performed back-to-back at the end-of-the-session concert. The first band was full of very capable musicians. They nailed their arrangements, never played a wrong chord, the drummer kept good time, and the vocalist sang in tune. Unfortunately, they got up on stage and stared at their feet the entire show. The audience politely clapped after each song.

The next band, a group of young, rambunctious boys who were friends outside of the program, proceeded to butcher just about every song they played. They didn't end a single song together, made arrangement mistakes all over the place, kept uneven time, and the guitar solos sounded like a bunch of meandering wanking. But they played with an incredible intensity, literally bouncing up and down on the stage. The lead singer strutted back and forth like Mick Jagger, and the guitar players rubbed up against one another back-to-back during their solos. The drummer hit hard and played with bombast. The audience went crazy for it.

I have seen this kind of scenario play out many times. I cannot overstate how important it is to own what you play and to try to play it like it's the *baddest*, most killing part anyone has ever played on that song. When you believe in what you're playing, the audience does too. When you play meekly or apologetically, the audience feels sorry for you and it makes for an uncomfortable listening experience.

Similarly, we once had a group of TV news broadcasters participate in a BandWorks session. The band was a group of rank amateurs, but, because of their television backgrounds, they all had tremendous stage presence. The lead singer worked the audience like a total pro, and the entire band looked like there was nowhere they'd rather be than rocking their hearts out onstage for the entire set. In that department, they blew away any band that has ever participated in the program. Musically, they weren't all that accomplished. I remember the drummer took a 4-minute solo, which is a risky undertaking even for the world's best drummers. This guy could barely play in time, but he got up and walked around the drum kit, playing it from behind with his back to the audience and the lights flashing. People ate it up.

I'm not trying to suggest that showmanship is more important than substance (and, in truth, both of these bands were playing for an audience of family and friends predisposed to be supportive), or that you can make up for poor quality music with high theatrics. But people respond to intensity and presence more than just about anything.

It's not easy to have this kind of confidence. You can't just manufacture it. But there are things you can do to help yourself move in that direction. For starters, *practice*. There's no better way to gain confidence in what you play than for it to feel second nature. If you find that you have to really concentrate to play your part, you're not there yet. If you need to look at the lyrics while you're singing, it's pretty difficult to deliver them with any emotion. If you need to watch your fingers on the fretboard, it's much more challenging to play the lick with any stage presence. If you're thinking about your bass drum pedal technique while you're playing a groove, it's almost impossible to deliver it with a good musical feel. So learn your parts and practice them until they become second nature, and you can focus your attention on things other than just playing the right notes.

Sometimes however, practicing isn't enough; it can take a mental adjustment. Even the most accomplished artists are sometimes plagued by self-doubt. (Ringo went through a well-documented crisis of confidence.) It's natural and understandable to have moments or periods of insecurity, but you can't live there if you want to sound good. So what can you do?

Consider why you got into playing in the first place—because it was *fun*. Remember to enjoy playing. You've worked so hard to get to this point, and you're performing in front of a live audience. Be present and not in your critical mind. If you have critical thoughts, or the doubts creep in while you're playing, notice them, and let them go by. Don't let them stay with you and don't get down on yourself for having them. Instead, train yourself to use these insidious thoughts as triggers to remind you to focus back on the music.

Occasionally, I still experience these doubts when I am playing. I've taught myself to use them as a reminder that if I am thinking about my right-foot technique, or the record label A&R guy in the audience, or the fact that I can't hear my toms in the mix, I am not focusing on what I should be—the *music*, and the *moment*. Almost all these things are outside of my control. My playing, and my focus, are within my control.

It takes time to retrain your brain to think positive thoughts about your playing instead of negative ones. And the change can be transformative, both in your playing and in how you feel about your playing. As you can see by now, these two things are related.

Another thing you can do is to sit down after a show and write down all the things you can remember that went through your mind while you were playing—particularly the negative ones, the feelings of doubt and insecurity. Give them their due, and let them look you back in the face after you write them down. Sometimes you'll be struck by how absurd they are. Other times you may find a nugget of something important that you need to work on.

Remember, you are who you were before you got to the show. You don't become a better or worse player immediately once you step on the stage. Your strengths and your weaknesses are always on display. Performing is a step in the process, not the end. There is always the next show.

Every time you perform on stage, strive to play as if what you're playing is the best part anyone has ever played. Play like every note is the most beautiful sounding note you've ever heard. It may sound corny, but if you can really arrive there, it can be incredibly liberating. All of a sudden, there are no mistakes, no expectations through which you can disappoint yourself. Your playing is you, and you are your playing. Not good or bad, just real. That's when the best music happens.

It can take some people many years to really arrive at the point where they feel like they can own what they play. Many never get there at all, or they experience only brief glimpses of it. Think of every performance as an opportunity to work on this—not to play perfectly, but to play honestly and with conviction and integrity. The best musicians know that this is the goal of every performance.

The most memorable shows I've ever been to were the ones where the band played their hearts out with terrific intensity and chemistry, and the connection with the audience was authentic and palpable. And while developing your skills will help build your confidence, every musician is capable of taking ownership of their playing at every stage of the game. Just think of those young teens who rocked the house. I still remember that show with a smile on my face.

ATTITUDE

The attitude a drummer plays with has an enormous effect on the band's overall sound. As the arbiter of the dynamics of the band, the drummer sets the tone and personality of each song with the energy and intensity with which he or she plays.

Furthermore, how a drummer plays can even affect how the other musicians play: when a drummer digs in and plays with conviction, it can make the other musicians in the band play better. With the groove strong and unfaltering, it takes the pressure off of the other musicians, who can relax into the song, confident the time is rock steady and supported by the integrity of the unwavering groove. Attitude begets attitude. A drummer playing with intensity will inspire his or her bandmates to bring the same.

Conversely, if a drummer plays meekly, the whole band feels like it lacks integrity. That's not to say louder is always better; you can still play with terrific intensity and presence without making people reach for the earplugs. I've seen drummers play with a fierce attitude but still keep their volume controlled. Loud or soft, you've got to play with conviction.

I once taught a band of teenagers with two drummers who shared duties on the kit. One was 12 years old, and a technically accomplished player. He could sightread charts note for note, had great time, and a huge vocabulary of grooves and fills. The other was 14 and had less experience, with a much smaller vocabulary and less refined technique. He didn't try to emulate the parts on the original recordings (he couldn't play them with his more rudimentary skill set), and his time was not as good as that of the younger drummer. But he hit the drums hard and played with great energy.

At the concert performance, the band played well, and both drummers did a great job. An adult musician in the program approached me as the band filed off stage. "Wow," he said, "That drummer was awesome!" "I know," I replied, "That little guy is such a solid player. He really nailed those parts." "No," he answered. "I mean the older one. He was killing it!" I nodded. He had killed it. The 14-year-old, with numerous hiccups in his playing, played with an energy and vitality that the younger drummer lacked. He lit a spark that all the band members responded to, and he made everyone around him play with more energy. He played with heart, and the audience felt it. The younger drummer nailed all the grooves and fills, but he lacked the presence to make the music really have an impact.

I once saw a very famous rock band play at the Fillmore in San Francisco. They had four guitar players on stage the entire night, all great players. There was one guitarist whose solos were particularly melodic, but I enjoyed them more when I closed my eyes, because the guy looked like he was having a miserable time up on stage. His face was expressionless, and he stared blankly down at the stage as he played. He had no stage presence at all, and seemed like he wasn't really there in his body. After the show, I was discussing the show with my friends, who unanimously thought the guitar player in question was not very good. They were responding to his energy, or lack thereof. I defended him half-heartedly, suggesting that what he played sounded good, even if he didn't seem like he was into it. But my friends were having none of it—they thought his attitude sucked and his playing reflected it. It was hard to argue with them.

INTENTION

When I was in college, I befriended one of my young professors, a Native American Studies teacher. Once every while we'd go grab a beer together, and one day we discovered that we both played softball. We agreed to get out and hit the ball around, and on a couple of occasions we made it out to a baseball field at Burns Park in Ann Arbor, taking turns hitting each other grounders and pop flies. The first time we went out, I saw that every time I hit the ball to him, no matter how difficult a play, he would go all out to try to make it. He would dive left and right trying to snag hard-hit grounders, scraping up his knees as he lunged for the ball. When we took a break, I asked him why he was trying so hard when we were just out to hit the ball around and have fun. "I always play 100%," he replied. "It's just the way I play. That way, I don't have to summon the intensity when it's game time. It's already hard-wired into me that I give my full effort all the time."

It gave me pause. I've since had similar experiences with other drummers. Steve Bowman, the original drummer in the band The Counting Crows (who also happened to play softball) told me the same thing about his drumming: "When I sit down to play, I always play with the intention of sounding as good as I can. I never play carelessly." He told me he'd learned that lesson from David Garibaldi.

I believe in the power of *intention*. A positive and focused mind-set can make a huge difference in the performance of any skill. The more you train yourself to play with intention, the more natural it becomes to always play that way; it doesn't become something you have to tap into, but becomes your automatic mode of operation.

I try to remember that every time I sit down to play the drums. I experience the same thing with both golf and archery, where in order to score well, you have to focus intently on every single shot, one at a time over the course of many attempts. It's challenging to always play with intention. It seems to me this is a lifelong pursuit.

HOW YOU PLAY IS USUALLY MORE IMPORTANT THAN WHAT YOU PLAY

Frequently, my students ask me to show them "the beat" to a certain song. I always encourage my students to come in with music that excites or interests them, and I love it when they come in with a groove they want to figure out or a fill they need help transcribing. Whenever people ask me about playing "the beat" to a song, I remind them that what they're really asking for is to learn what a particular drummer did on a particular recording. While it's true that many drummers who perform live will play the same part that was on the original recording, it's also true that many drummers will play a slightly different part when performing live.

There are occasions when a drum part or fill has become so iconic to a song that to alter it is to risk redefining the song. The Beatles' "Come Together" comes to mind, or the intro fill in "(She's a) Brick House," although even those songs have been covered by bands with different grooves. (Check out the Meters' version of "Come Together," it's super groovy and very different from the original.) For the most part, drummers can play a range of different things when they play live and still make the song sound great while staying true to the character of the song. In other words, there is no "right" part to play.

If you asked five of the world's best drummers to sit down and play a song they'd never heard, they would all play something different. In all likelihood, they would bring similar *qualities* to their playing, and their parts might even end up sounding similar—but they would all be different, either in content or delivery, or both. Which goes to prove that there is no *correct* part to play, only parts that are more musical or less musical, which is of course a somewhat subjective determination.

Most of the time, when I teach someone a song, we will start by trying to emulate the drum part from the recording. There is great value in learning from the pros. You can pick up licks and ideas, and if you do it enough, you can start to develop your own musical instincts for what to play. Before we move on from a song, I ask my students to play the song without reading a chart or copying a part. I want them to play it how they would want to play it, or to at least explore what that might sound like. "Nobody is going to be sitting in the audience judging your performance based on how true to the recording it is," I advise them. "Nobody even knows the original drum part. And even if they did, you could easily play it note for note and still not sound any good if you don't play with good feel. So what do you need to bring to this tune to make it work?"

I ask them for specifics. Usually they'll describe the drum part as it is on the recording. "Is that really what you need?" I ask.

I try a different tack: "Imagine you're the drummer in the band, and just as you're walking up on stage, you slip and sprain your ankle, and you can't play. I'm sitting there in the wings and can sub for you, but I've never heard the song before. What are you going to tell me in 30 seconds that I need to know to play the song?" This gets them thinking a little differently. If they respond with a particular bass drum part, I may challenge them: "So you're saying I have to play that part exactly? It wouldn't work if I played a different part?" Or I'll redirect: "What is the song about? What's the energy of the song like? The mood? What's the role of the drums? Are there any arrangement things I need to know about, like breaks or dynamics?" Essentially, I'm trying to get them thinking more about *how* to play (maybe 75–80%) than *what* to play (maybe 20–25%).

Together we try to distill down the essence of the song and think about what's really most important about how the drums function in the context of the song. When they've made some headway on the answer, I'll ask them to take their own advice and play the song keeping only those things in mind as priorities and to let go of copying the part on the recording. They tend to play more relaxed, a little looser than when they're trying to play something so specific. And more importantly, they begin to gain the confidence that what they can offer creatively can be musically valid, and they can begin to trust their own instincts.

KEEP IT SIMPLE

I've been teaching at Cazadero Performing Arts Family Camp every year since 1996. "Caz Family Camp" is a weeklong retreat where kids and adults can take classes in all manner of instruments and participate in various ensembles up in the redwoods of Northern California.

One year, there was an accomplished guest violinist and teacher at the camp. One of the classes she was offering was called K.I.S.S., which stood for "Keep It Simple, Stupid!" Curious, I sat in on her class one day, which turned out to be mostly about improvisation. She laid down a simple blues progression and had people take turns improvising over it one chorus at a time. Then she'd offer feedback, which was mostly along the lines of "Keep it simple… simpler! Let me hear your phrasing so clearly that I could sing back to you what you played!"

It worked. People had started out trying to play lines that they thought were sophisticated. They imagined that soloing needed to be complicated, since they'd heard so many accomplished musicians play such complex stuff. As they pared down their ideas and the corresponding number of notes, they began to play more bluesy and lyrical riffs, with cleaner phrasing, and they sounded more musical.

The teacher didn't say anything about which notes people should play, though it seemed most people knew their pentatonic scales. Nor did she bring up dynamics, but somehow the simpler people played, the more dynamically they played. I was amazed how this single piece of advice made such a positive difference in how people approached improvising.

IT'S EASIER TO ADD THAN TO TAKE AWAY

A good dish is easily ruined by over-seasoning it. That's why cooks learn to add spices a little bit at a time when experimenting with a new recipe. When seasoning for flavor, a little bit can go a long way.

As a drummer, if you're playing too little, it's easy to hear that the music could use more—it feels too spare or thin and begs for more robust playing, more rhythmic support, or dynamism. If you're playing too much, it just sounds full, and it's much more difficult to recognize how the music might sound better with less going on. I always try to start with simpler parts, then get more sophisticated if I think the music warrants it. I don't think I've ever heard a non-drummer complain that a drum part was too simple.

A few years ago, I watched a video of a Steve Gadd clinic. Steve is one of the most recorded rock and pop drummers of all time, and he is widely known for his impeccable feel, instincts, and creativity. In it, there was a Q&A session where members of the audience got to ask Steve questions about his music and philosophy. One of the guests aptly credited Steve with having worked with hundreds of famous artists, and being the first-call drummer for recording sessions among the top musicians of our generation. He went on to ask what Steve's general approach is when he goes into the studio. Steve replied something like, "After listening to the lyrics and trying to understand the intent and vibe of the song, I basically try to play as simply as I can. I find that the simpler I play, the easier it is to keep time."

It sounds so self-evident. I would add that the simpler you play, the easier it is to hear if it sounds good. Layers are more exposed, you can hear whether things are fitting together more clearly, and it's easier to tell if your part should be more robust. Steve's advice is spot on, naturally. And it goes to show why he has played on hundreds of well-known albums (and on some of them, his playing is anything but simple).

Several years ago, one of my students attended PIT (The Percussion Institute of Technology) in Southern California, where they've had some very reputable teachers on the faculty. He told me that in one of his classes, there was an assignment to play along to a recorded rock or pop song without playing even one fill. Just groove. Most of the students failed the assignment on the first try. They couldn't help themselves from playing fills. It's just so much easier to overplay than underplay.

Drummers learn early on to play fills, and we work hard to develop instincts for when and how to play them. What a fantastic exercise for an advanced drummer to play an entire song without playing any fills at all. If you try it, you'll notice where you want to play fills, and you can actually learn to make better choices about what fills to play; you'll hear exactly what's missing.

LET IT BE

A few years ago, I played a string of gigs with a really great piano player, one of the top jazz players in the Bay Area. He lived up to his reputation, demonstrating impressive command of the instrument, his playing always fluid and full of great ideas. The only problem was that he felt a compulsion to express so many of those ideas at almost every opportunity, and even sometimes when there was no opportunity. He would never let anything sit and groove and just sound good where it was. There was always some unexpected twist he had to add: a harmonic suggestion, a rhythmic displacement… something to show off either his limitless fountain of ideas or his ample chops, or both. The guy was indisputably a monster player. But the music never felt relaxed, and we were never able to get into a mood or groove because he wouldn't *let it be*.

It's taken me a long time to develop my instincts for what not to play. Even now I sometimes forget, get caught up in the moment and throw some distracting permutation or wayward idea into the music that was better left in my head. At first, it's a matter of learning to quiet those instincts to play something that, upon hearing it out loud, doesn't fit. Over time, you actually develop the instinct for what does fit, and those errant ideas occur to you less and less frequently.

Most mainstream Western music has fairly simple drum parts. Even when the parts are more sophisticated, they tend not to move around too much. After all, for music to be easy to dance to, it has to have a regular and consistent beat. This is not a value judgment. There is a lot of great music (that not as many people listen to) with drumming that is both complex and dynamic, constantly changing from measure to measure—look no further than the music of jazz greats Elvin Jones, Max Roach, or Tony Williams. But even in jazz, prog-rock, or fusion, there is often a feeling of sameness, a relaxed percolating or churning that has a calmness and consistency, a *groove*, even in its dynamism. This is not easily achieved. *The more complex and dynamic the part, the harder it is to create the feeling of groove.* It takes a very accomplished player to pull it off without sacrificing the integrity of the music.

There will be occasions when a situation may call for a stream-of-consciousness kind of approach, where the drummer may be encouraged to fill up space with a lot of ideas as they occur to him. These occasions are rare. More of the time, your best bet is to find the groove and the vibe, and let it be.

THE WRONG AND THE RIGHT MOTIVATION

When I was a teenager and had worked my way through The Funky Primer *(a great book of rock and funk grooves by Charles Dowd), my goal was to play as complicated as I could at every opportunity. I thought that the more complex my drum beats, the better I sounded.* Surely people will recognize how good I am when they hear me play this beat! *I would think. I see this sometimes with my students, and I tell them my own story to try to disavow them of this absurd notion.*

I like to think of the Hippocratic Oath applying to drumming just as it does to medicine: First, do no harm.

Choosing to play something based on how complex it is—or to want to be noticed—*only serves your ego. It rarely makes the music sound better. On the contrary, overplaying mainly serves to obfuscate the groove and dilute the emotional impact of the song. When I was younger, I am sure I didn't notice other players doing this as much, since I was in my own world, trying to do it myself. Now I can hear it a mile away. It doesn't feel like much of a musical experience really, but more of an exercise in playground one-upsmanship. I try to teach my students to avoid this pitfall.*

You must always remember that your playing is part of something bigger, and you have a responsibility to the larger whole that you are creating with other players. The audience is experiencing the entire sound, the whole package of what you are trying to deliver with your fellow musicians. And though the drummer plays a critical role, it's not all about the drums *(it's also about the vocals!).*

Everything you play should be motivated by what you

hear. If you're choosing what to play based on wanting people to think you're good, or because your drum teacher is in the audience, or that cute girl or boy you want to impress is listening, you are only serving your insecurity, your ego. To the best of your ability, focus on the music, and stay faithful to your interpretation of what the music is asking of you. You will always sound better when you do.

THINKING OUTSIDE THE BOX

One of the assignments I occasionally give my more advanced students is to come in each week having composed two or three new beats or riffs that they have transcribed. I'm frequently stunned by the creativity and diversity of what they bring in.

We often marvel at drummers like Jim Keltner and Kenny Buttrey for coming up with eminently creative and unique parts to songs, and rightfully so. Who would have thought to play Keltner's brilliant broken-groove drumming on Ry Cooder's "Cherry Ball Blues"? Or Buttrey's singular bongo-and-ashtray-playing-part on Bob Dylan's "Lay Lady Lay"? I would assert that many of my students' creations rival those parts in their creativity and uniqueness. Of course, in the end it's all about the part fitting the song. Sometimes songs can even be built around drum parts instead of the other way around. So, I tell my students to keep some of their grooves in their pockets in case an opportunity ever arises to fit it with a song, or even write a song around it. The main point of the exercise is to explore different ways of conceiving drum parts: to consider different sequences and patterns that are not standard or conventional, and to hear how these different textures can shape a song in a unique way.

The more you explore coming up with differently conceived

parts, the more comfortable you become thinking unconventionally and creatively in musical situations. If you're used to coming up with interesting musical ideas, you start to hear them in your head more frequently, and more different things will occur to you to play. This is not to suggest that your job as a drummer is always to come up with the most creative part you can; often the simplest part is the best. But there are times when you can really shape the disposition of a song with an unconventional approach.

PUSHING THE ENVELOPE

One of the most effective exercises I employ when teaching bands is what I call the "Scale of 1 to 10 Exercise." It's a remarkably simple and effective way to help bands learn to push the envelope of dynamics and intensity. When a band isn't playing with enough oomph or authority, I'll ask them to try to exaggerate the intensity with which they play. "Pretend you're playing this song like a heavy metal song," I suggest. "Play it way over the top. Exaggerate how strong you play it to the point of it sounding totally inappropriate." In giving them permission to let loose and just have fun with it, they end up digging in more and play with more conviction.

"OK," I'll tease them, "that was a good start. Let's imagine on a scale of 1 to 10, that was approaching a 5. Can we take it up to 10?"

Conversely, I'll also try to get them to dial down the volume, to play at a whisper, down to a 1. And then lower, as softly as they can play and still be audible. Sometimes I'll turn off the lights to encourage it further.

I've witnessed amazing things happen from this exercise: I've heard bands explore a dynamic range they didn't know was possible. And, I've seen bands completely change their approach to playing a tune, infusing it with a totally different feel than before, pushing their music to a higher plane.

Engaging in the "scale of 1 to 10" exercise is a way to help musicians realize how much more is possible, how they can push themselves beyond limits to places they didn't know they were capable of going. It can also serve to help a band nail down exactly where they want to play a song in terms of dynamics or feel. It's the same concept recording engineers use when they're mixing in the studio: they'll turn up or down a dimension of the EQ or effect on a track—or the volume of it—past the point of where it sounds good to their ears, just to hear what's too much or too little, only then to bring it back to within the range of what sounds good.

VERSATILITY

When I was in my twenties, I believed that to be a professional drummer you had to be capable in a wide range of styles of music: jazz, rock, blues, Latin, hip-hop, funk, reggae, and a few others. Now with the advent of various sub-genres such as psych-pop, trip-hop, acid jazz, neo-soul, drum & bass, and more, there are even more styles important to know. While I still think it's important to cover the big bases no matter which style(s) you end up playing, I'm more a believer in specializing than I used to be.

It's nearly impossible to be great at every one of these styles. All you need to do is listen to someone who is steeped in hard bop to know that you need to live and breathe that music to become *really* accomplished at it. Or check out a trap drummer in a samba group to realize that Brazil has an incredibly rich and diverse musical history all its own that could take a lifetime to explore. There are videos, tomes, and seemingly endless resources to help you dig into any style or sub-genre of music and drumming.

If you listen to Motown and R&B and play in a couple of those types of bands, you will get good at playing those styles. If you are a devotee of New Orleans music and study second line and funk drumming, you will develop proficiency at that. Within every discipline is the possibility to highly specialize, and get very, very good at one kind of thing.

So while I do recommend that all drummers learn to play jazz, rock, pop, Latin, hip-hop, reggae, and funk (to name the most commonly played styles), in the long run, you should pursue what turns you on. Play the music you have passion for. Ultimately, your drumming will sound best when you're playing what you love to play.

KNOW YOUR ROLE

Like an actor in a play or an athlete on a team, as a drummer you need to know your role. What style of music are you playing? How much creative space do you have to stretch out? Naturally, you shouldn't assume that because you normally like to play aggressively that that means every situation calls for heavy playing. Generally speaking, the smaller the group, the more room you have to fill up space. The larger the group, the more likely you're going to be stepping on someone's toes or taking up too much sonic space in the mix.

I once played a handful of gigs with a seven-piece band that included a pedal steel player. I remember being surprised at how little the pedal steel player played. When he did play, it always sounded great. I told him as much, and encouraged him to play more. He replied that there wasn't much room for him, and that as it was he felt like he was squeezing in wherever he could. As soon as he said it, it made total sense. Part of what made his playing sound so good was that he was adding it in just the right spots. Too much, and you wouldn't have noticed how special it was. It wasn't obtrusive, and it always came just when the music needed a fill or melodic line to fill in the space left by the vocal. Sometimes having just enough of one flavor is the thing. Too much and you've ruined the experience.

RINGO

Astonishingly, there continues to be a great debate in the drumming community about whether Ringo Starr is a good drummer. I'll say it again: being a good drummer is about so much more than having chops and technique. It's about finding just the right musical part to play and delivering it with the feel appropriate to the song. Good drum parts don't go along with the song; they are the song. They are a critical part of the whole and have a huge impact on the overall character and delivery of the music. And if that is the criteria by which we measure good drummers, then Ringo is one of the all-time best.

Another drummer could easily have overplayed so many of those great Beatles songs, or played them too heavy-handed, or crowded them with too many fills. Ringo played with a simplicity and unpretentious delivery that defined many of those songs. He knew when to hold back and let the melodies and textures stand front and center (on songs like "Sun King"), and when to drive hard (on songs like "A Hard Day's Night") and when to add his distinct creativity (like with the dragging triplet beat on "Ticket to Ride").

The Beatles are widely considered the most important rock band of all time, and for good reason. They evolved dramatically over the 10 years they were together, and wrote song after brilliant song that, along with keen and creative production help from George Martin, became part of the fabric of people's lives for generations. How can you not hold Ringo up as one of the most musical drummers of all time? If it were just a matter of being in the right place at the right time, we'd be talking about Pete Best instead.

HEARING THE TAPESTRY

I have tremendous respect for arrangers and producers. They often get little recognition for their contribution to a recorded or performed work. The good ones have very finely-attuned ears and a multitude of reference points from listening to and working on so much music. And they have great instincts.

I went to see Jon Brion play at Largo in Los Angeles several years ago. Jon is a multi-instrumentalist, songwriter, singer, arranger, and producer who's worked with Aimee Mann (one of my favorite singer/ songwriters) and many other artists, and produced a number of movie soundtracks. It was a one-man show. Jon used loops to lay down multiple keyboard tracks, drums, guitars, and bass, then would get up and sing through the entirety of a song, fully arranged but pieced together in real time before the audience. It was like watching a master chef improvise a fully evolved multi-course meal off the top of his head. Often, I would have a difficult time imagining how a part he would start with would ultimately fit into the arrangement, but, sure enough, all of the parts he played—and there were often several keyboard and guitar parts for each song—blended into a brilliantly arranged whole. The songs sounded like they were produced through many weeks of layering in the studio, when each one only took about 5–10 minutes to assemble.

[At one point during the show, Jon asked the audience for song suggestions for him to play. For about a minute or two, people in the audience yelled out random songs. I thought he was waiting to hear something he wanted to play, until at one point he held up his hand and exclaimed, "OK! That's enough!" He then proceeded to play every single one of the 15 suggestions on the guitar, singing a verse and chorus of each song, fingerpicking most of them in a bluegrass style, segueing into each song effortlessly as if he had rehearsed it ten times. It was awe-inspiring.]

Like many great producers, Jon has the ears and instincts to hear the finished piece with all its layers and subtleties before it's fully assembled. In this case, he was able to play the parts that were in his head, rather than try to pull them out of musicians or add layers on top of what they were playing.

This ability to "hear the tapestry" is an invaluable quality in a musician. Understanding how parts fit together to make the whole is such a crucial part of making good music, especially as it grows more complex. While there may be exquisite beauty in the simplicity of a 4-track recording of guitar and vocals (Iron & Wine and Cat Stevens come to mind), there is also great artistry in Phil Spector's lush Wall of Sound, which at times was comprised of over 100 separate tracks. Or Berry Gordy's perfectly arranged Motown records, or the modern pop and hip-hop albums, which often have several dozen tracks layered upon one another.

George Martin has often been referred to as the "5th Beatle," and rightfully so. With his classical background, George was able to contribute integral parts to many of the Beatles' songs, adding sophisticated layers to the arrangements which pushed the songs far beyond what the band had originally conceived. Along with his help, the band began to use the recording studio as an instrument in its own right, producing songs and even entire albums that could not be performed live. It was the beginning of a whole new way of making recorded music that would influence bands for decades to come. It also at once engendered and defined the role of the modern-era producer, and paved the way for future musicians to become artist/producers themselves, adding all the finishing touches on their own without the aid of an additional specialist.

I like to think about the role of the producer when I play drums with singer/songwriters and on creative projects, and imagine myself as the drummer and producer at the same time. The devil is in the details after all, so it makes good sense for the drummer to carefully consider his contribution to a musical piece and how it blends into the context of the whole.

SERVING THE MUSIC

Hal Blaine, the primary percussionist in producer Phil Spector's Wall of Sound, leader of the legendary L.A. studio band referred to as "The Wrecking Crew," and likely the most recorded drummer of the 20th century (over 35,000 recordings, including 150 Top-10 hits and 40 #1 hits), once said, "I'm not a flashy drummer. I want to be a great accompanist."

Great drummers have great instincts, and their instincts direct them to play what sounds good in context of the whole. *A lot of drummers can come up with interesting drum parts on their own. It's the rare player who has a vision for adding something creative to the mix that ultimately defines the song, the way Steve Gadd's brilliant marching cadence-inspired groove does on Paul Simon's "50 Ways to Leave Your Lover," or how his Mozambique-flavored Latin groove hits the mark on "Late in the Evening." For the most part, Gadd's grooves (to use one example of a great, musical drummer) don't particularly stand out. When he plays with Eric Clapton or James Taylor, his playing doesn't draw attention (other than for his deft touch and deep pocket), because the music doesn't ask for it. If he played something that stood out in those contexts, he would draw attention away from the singing or the guitar playing and distract from the emotional intent and vibe of the song.*

Of course, it can be a matter of debate as to which musical choices a drummer makes serve the music and which don't. It's not always clear or obvious. It might be difficult for a listener to put his or her finger on what isn't working about a song, whereas an experienced drummer might be able to discern that a part may be too busy, or too heavy, or that the snare drum doesn't have enough pop to drive the band's sound. A drummer (really, every musician) needs to depend on her instincts to play a good part and to deliver it with the right sensitivity to the situation—from whisper soft brushes to head-banging death metal. She has to listen to the other parts, suss out the layers of rhythms and dynamics, and give the song the right musical vibe or quality.

When a drum part works, it becomes a part of the music, not something added on or played along with, much the same way as when a cook adds a flavor into a dish, it can infuse the whole with a new identity. The new flavor can become a fundamental part of the dish, even defining it, or it can be subtler, adding a hint of something exotic; or it can help to enhance and complement other flavors that may taste different in combination. A good drummer, like a good chef, knows how ingredients interact and influence each other, and creates her parts with the whole in mind.

MIKE CLARK'S CHEESEBURGER

One of my friends told me a great story about Mike Clark, the underappreciated funk and jazz drummer who played with Herbie Hancock's Headhunters (among many illustrious others), and is one of the most sampled funk drummers in contemporary music. I'd seen Mike at a clinic a couple of years earlier and was struck by his sincerity and lack of pretentiousness. He said of all the styles of music he plays, his favorite is to play a deep, grooving shuffle—one that doesn't go anywhere, but just sits in an unwavering pocket. He said he could play that all night long. For all his chops and linear drumming mastery, the guy just wants to play shuffles all day. You gotta love that. Mike also said that he never practices without playing along with music. Food for thought....

At another clinic Mike was giving (this one to a group of young drummers at a summer camp where each student was on his own drum kit), Mike asked each drummer, one at a time, to play his or her version of a funky groove. Each student played for a few bars, mostly with a lot of syncopation and complexity. Then Mike sat down and said, "Now listen to this. This is why I'm going to steal your gig," he said playfully. And he proceeded to lay it down, *simple*, *phat* and *funky*. He went on to talk about the sound he gets when he hits the snare drum, how he digs the stick into the drum and holds it there, without a rebound, the opposite of how every drummer is taught to play.

He explained, "When I hit the snare drum, I want it to feel like the listener is biting into a big, juicy cheeseburger, and the grease is running down their face because the groove is so thick and greasy." The point is well taken. So many young drummers don't hit the snare with any authority. They swipe at it with a "J" motion, hitting the drum with a glancing stoke, and fail to generate any crack or pop on the backbeat.

I love to tell this story to my students. He told a similar story at the clinic I attended about playing with the legendary blues guitarist Albert Collins, who stopped a rehearsal to implore Mike to "Put some chicken fat on the groove!" and even kicked Mike off the kit for a minute to show him how. Chicken fat, grease, filth, nastiness...it's all the same thing. It comes from a feeling of inexorable *grooviness*, an indefatigable consistency of time and tone, the right balance of tone and volume from each part of the kit, together providing the propulsion that makes the song move.

At times, I can implore students for a half hour to try to get them to hit the drums—or even just the hi-hat—a certain way. We can break down the angle of the stick attack, the location on the cymbal, the grip and stroke, the left foot pressure. Often that's helpful, but sometimes it only goes so far. There's a certain amount of it that is analyzable and a certain dimension that defies analysis. To get to that part, to help students muster the right intensity in their funk grooves, sometimes the cheeseburger does the trick.

GETTING INTO CHARACTER

I worked with a drum student for a number of years who went on to study acting at a prestigious program in England. He was an extremely bright and sensitive young man, whose enthusiasm for drums was second only to his passion for acting. We were talking one day about the similarities between acting and drumming, about the notion of *getting into character* both for different acting roles and for playing drums on different songs. For many drummers, an intuitive sense of feel comes only from many years spent practicing and playing various styles of music, and from listening to hundreds or even thousands of recordings. But there are a number of shortcuts you can take to attaining the appropriate feel for a song if you pay attention to what the song is asking you to do, and you have some degree of independent dynamic and rhythmic control of your limbs.

Unfortunately for some amateur drummers, they approach many subtly (or sometimes even not too subtly) different songs with the same concept and dynamic. They rely on a handful of trusted, comfortable beats that they can play fairly well at a consistent tempo and volume. Often, they inhibit their ability to bring out the musical potential of a composition by falling back on their limited vocabulary. But even more often, drummers fail to define the song with a good musical feel from a lack of listening and a dearth of musical sensitivity; in essence, a failure to get into character.

Most professional drummers know instinctively that every song calls for its own technical, conceptual, and musical approach. They also know that how they play is just as important as what they play.

I've heard so many intermediate drummers in BandWorks play parts just as they're written, note for note, mechanically faithful to the original recording. But even they admit that they sound nothing like those great drummers they're trying to emulate. So what gives? How can two drummers playing the same part at the same tempo sound completely different? How can one drummer sound so much better?

It's not the drums—it's the *feel*. Most of us have heard this word before, or maybe even used it when we didn't completely understand it. Playing with a good feel for a song has to do with finding the right musical character, the right attitude or feeling for a song to make it sound good, the same way an actor must artfully deliver a line to convey the right emotion to make a scene work. And truthfully, if you sat down five great drummers to play the same song, they might all play with a slightly different feel. But they would all sound good; there is no "right" part to play, there is no "correct" feel. But there are lots of ways to sound more musical or less so.

One of the difficulties in defining *feel* is that it's really a feeling that you're trying to translate into the drum part and imbue the song with a certain character. How can you play the drums to make a song sound darker or brighter? Or make it chug along more? Or have a more Caribbean flavor, for example? You've got to learn to translate feelings into sounds. A darker sound could mean more toms and low cymbal sounds; bright can mean a tight hi-hat and popping snare; chugging along could mean playing more on top of the beat, or adding snare notes to give more of a moving train kind of vibe; a more Caribbean feel could involve a rim click, cymbal bell, and movement around the toms. There are no rules about how to make a groove feel a certain way. Experiment to find out what works for you, and explore the sonic possibilities of your kit. And listen to a lot of music.

Naturally, part of sounding good has to do with coming up with a good part, i.e. choosing what to play. If you pay careful attention to the rhythmic parts you're hearing from the rest of the band, you're more likely to come up with a drum part that makes rhythmic sense. You need to have an understanding of how your four-limbed part fits rhythmically with the bass line, the rhythm guitar part, the keyboard part, etc. in order to make a decision about how to best complement the other parts you're hearing. Is it best to mirror the bass part with the bass drum? Or weave them together with some overlap? Should the snare stay on 2 and 4, or should you play it more syncopated, or with ghost notes to fill out the groove? By increasing your vocabulary as a drummer, you'll have more ideas to choose from to create parts that work well. And by listening to more music, you'll develop better instincts for what sounds good and feels good.

But playing a musical drum part is about more than just picking the right notes to play. Most great drum parts stand out from good ones in the way that they're played. Does the pocket swing? To what degree? Should the groove be played on top of the beat, square in the middle, or slightly behind? How tight is the hi-hat? What part of the stick should you hit it with, and at which angle? There is a wide range of tightness/looseness you can achieve on the hi-hat with your left foot. Pressing down with just the right amount of tension can make all the difference. What kind of tone should you get out of the snare? Where should you hit the ride cymbal? These are the kinds of things that will help determine the overall sound of the drums and the character the drum part as a whole imparts to the song.

In Method Acting, an actor aspires to expressive and sincere performances by fully inhabiting the role of his or her character. Similarly, a drummer needs to know what motivates a drum part. Ask yourself what the song is about. You need to determine the mood, character, energy, and vibe. Is it about "Burning Down the House"? "Dancing in the Street"? Or "Sitting on the Dock of the Bay"? How can the drum part contribute to that musical intention? More broadly, what role do the drums play in the song? Is the drummer driving the bus, lighting the spark? Is it all about drums and vocal? Or maybe it's more about guitar and vocal, and the drums are mostly for rhythmic support? Pushing or laid back? Heavy or light? Busy or sparse? Dark and moody or bright and cheerful?

It can get daunting trying to analyze the character of a song and best determine how the drums fit into it. But you'll get better with practice and with feedback from your bandmates and your teachers. Over time, you'll get to the prize more and more quickly. Many top drummers can get into character without even thinking about it. Their instincts just lead them to the right groove with the right feel from the first downbeat. But for those of us without the incredible gifts of someone like Jim Keltner or Steve Gadd, taking a minute or two to think about your motivation for playing the tune can help you come up with a good musical approach.

* * *

The two most critical aspects to playing any popular song well on the drums are playing with a steady tempo and a consistent feel. If you have trouble keeping time, how well you play the feel is really of secondary importance—you have to maintain a steady tempo before you worry about anything else. But once you can play fairly steady, the next most important thing is maintaining a consistent feel. Part of this has to do with being physically relaxed when you play; part of it has to do with staying where you are on the front edge or back edge of the beat; and part of it has to do with maintaining a consistent sound. Every time you hit the snare on 2 & 4, it should sound the same. Your hi-hat should not get tighter and looser over the course of a groove unless you mean it to for dynamic effect. The bass drum should be played with the same attack and intention on each note unless you deliberately want to vary it to change the flow of the part. Playing the drums with consistent timbres on each part of the kit will go a long way toward making you sound steady, and can even improve the flow of your time.

[In jazz, drummers usually take a different approach, with each note having its own color and character, speaking more expressively. But with rock and dance music or anything with a repetitive groove, consistency of sound is paramount.]

Another aspect of playing with a good feel has to do with the energy you play with. I've heard so many drummers play parts that would sound great if they would just *hit* the drums. Confidence takes time to develop, but you'll never find it playing timidly and hiding behind the kit. Play every note like you mean it. Believe in your playing. Your goal is to sound good, and you don't sound good when you don't play with integrity. That's not to say louder is always better; you can still play with amazing intensity and presence without making people reach for the ear plugs. I've seen drummers play with a fierce attitude but still keep their volume controlled. Use rods or brushes, grip the sticks higher up, make shorter strokes, but always play your parts with intention.

SETTING THE DIALS

When most drummers think of dynamics, they usually consider how loud they play in relation to the other instruments in the band. Often overlooked is the importance of setting the dynamics of the parts of the drum kit relative to one other. How loud is the hi-hat compared to the snare drum? Is the bass drum punchy or just there for rhythmic support? How essential is it to the groove? Does the snare crack on the backbeat or is it played more in the middle of the mix? Does it make you want to shake your butt, clap your hands, or just snap your fingers? Think of this the way a recording engineer sets the dials or faders on a mixing board to create the perfect balance for the music.

It's remarkable how much of a difference the balance of the parts of the drum kit relative to one other can make in the overall feeling of the music. Just take the songs "Carolina in My Mind" by James Taylor (the version re-recorded on his Greatest Hits album), "Billie Jean" by Michael Jackson, and "Enter Sandman" by Metallica for example. The layperson would never guess that those three songs had the same basic drum beat, because they feel totally different. "Carolina..." is played by studio drummer Russ Kunkel with a light touch, with the hi-hat quiet relative to the snare, which is dry and focused. The drums are being played as rhythmic support for the vocal, giving the groove a light, airy feeling, and the back-side-of-the-beat leaning helps suit the song's slightly melancholy quality. "Billie Jean" is played by jazz great Ndugu Chancler, pretty square in the middle, with an even balance between the parts of the kit, a super dry hi-hat and bass drum sound, and a very focused snare attack (though there is a ton of reverb on it, which opens up the sound of the otherwise very dry drum beat). In contrast, "Enter Sandman" is played by Metallica co-founder Lars Ulrich with heaviness and bombast, a super loose and aggressive hi-hat that dominates the feel, heavy attack on the snare and kick, and a front-edge-of-the-beat lean, giving the song a visceral, driving intensity that makes it *Rock*. Three songs with the same drum part, but each delivered in a totally different manner.

When I coach students to play along with music, I'll often direct them to increase or decrease the presence or change the tone of a part, or parts, of the kit. It may mean playing 20% harder on the snare to give the groove more strength, or digging into the bass drum with just a little more force to fill out the bottom. It might mean reducing the foot pressure on the hi-hat ever so slightly to give the groove a more meaty sound, or changing the angle of attack of the stick on the hi-hat to make it cut. It could mean hitting the snare drum closer to the edge to lighten up the backbeat, or moving up three inches on the ride cymbal to get a drier, more focused sound; or relaxing the grip on the stick so the drum resonates more when struck. And so on. If they can't make these changes on command, we'll work on exercises to develop the freedom required to control each limb independently of the others. We'll also explore the varied sounds they can get from striking the drums and cymbals differently and with various implements and diverse techniques. It takes a long time to be able to manipulate your limbs with this degree of independent control, and it takes even longer to develop the ear and musical instincts to make musical decisions about how to "set the dials" in every musical situation.

These adjustments are the kinds of things that tend not to occur to the amateur drummer, who tends to sit down and play without much regard for the balance of the kit, both in terms of volume and tone. Developing the control and instincts to nail the feel of the song are vital to playing music with any sophistication.

Naturally, it makes a difference what instruments you choose to play. One's choice of drums, cymbals (especially), heads, and sticks will determine the sonic range of possibilities one can create. Just like pianos and wind instruments, drums and cymbals are endowed with several tonal characteristics that together make up the fundamental voice of the instrument. It is the musician's job to find that voice and make it sing.

Jazz drumming legend "Philly Joe" Jones said that "every cymbal is five cymbals," meaning there are a number of voices that every cymbal is capable of producing. (I'd assert that a cymbal has more than that, but they're not necessarily easy to produce consistently.) For drummers, the control lies in your hands and feet. It's your ear that helps you know how to set the dials for the perfect mix.

* * *

Here's a great exercise for developing more independent control of your limbs, greatly enhancing your ability to dial in your sound for a particular song and achieve a good, musical feel:

Start by practicing hitting two drums simultaneously, one note at a time, exaggerating the dynamic difference. Push the envelope as far as you can by playing the loud notes as loud as you possibly can and the soft notes as soft as possible. If you do it right, you should barely be able to hear the soft note at all. These kinds of exaggerated strokes, though perhaps not commonly used in musical situations, will enable you to easily play parts with a narrower range of dynamic contrast, more typical of real songs. Concentrate on hitting both limbs at exactly the same time.

I like to hit the right hand on the hi-hat, tightly closed (for soft) to very loose (for loud). Snare strokes should be near the edge (soft) to center (loud). Bass drum strokes should be heel down (soft) to heel up (loud).

RH = Right Hand   LH = Left Hand   RF = Right Foot

STEP 1: Two limbs at a time

SOFT	LOUD
RH	LH
RH	RF
LH	RH
LH	RF
RF	RH
RF	LH

STEP 2: Three limbs at a time

SOFT	LOUD
RH	LH + RF
LH	RH + RF
RF	RH + LH
RH + LH	RF
RH + RF	LH
LH + RF	RH

STEP 3:

Play the above combinations in Step 2 with a
simple rock beat instead of just one note at a time.

Once you can play a simple groove with any of the above dynamic combinations, see if you can make more subtle dynamic changes, like adding 20% more volume on the snare, or pulling the bass drum back just a little in the mix. Then you can try some more complicated beats, but keep the focus on maintaining a smooth tempo and accurate dynamic control.

Chances are if you're listening to one of your favorite bands, the drummer is very good. Learn from him or her. Listen to songs with a focus on the sound of the drum parts that you hear; notice which part(s) of the kit are most prominent. If you're trying to cop the groove, try to imitate the dynamic balance of the parts of the kit. You'll often hear an immediate improvement in your playing.

ELVIN JONES

I was 16 when I saw Elvin Jones and his Jazz Machine for the first time at the Blue Note in New York City. I sat at the table right in front of the band, three feet away from his bass drum. My head swayed back and forth as I listened to him play with such ferocity and power, leading the band like a possessed shaman dancing in rapture of the holy spirit of jazz. I walked out of the club dizzy from the experience. I didn't understand most of it, but it blew my mind.

I would see Elvin many more times before he died, and got to chat with him on a handful of occasions. He was always generous, happy to take whatever time he could in-between sets or after the gig to talk to people who wanted to talk to him. I think he was one of the most important and influential jazz drummers of all time. A genius and an innovator, he conceptualized jazz punctuation phrased in triplets; the "circle of sound," as his playing was character- ized, unlike his predecessors who mostly thought in pairs of 8th notes. He painted with vivid artistry, often describ- ing the sounds and phrases he heard and played in terms of color and texture. Along with Coltrane, he brought the music to a new spiritual plane.

After seeing him at Blues Alley in Washington, D.C., I wrote this poem for Elvin. I ended up handing him a copy of it some years later. He accepted it graciously, and I am sure that he read it, but I never heard anything from him, and he died before I could see him again. I hope he felt the admira- tion I felt for him. I didn't really know him personally, but from our limited interactions, and from reading and watching interviews with him, he struck me as a magnanimous soul.

THE LAST TIME I SAW ELVIN JONES

Was at Blues Alley in Washington, D.C.
The candles flickered, applauding
With every crash and smash and boom and shimmer.
Yes, yes, I heard them say yes, yes, and they whistled
Because Elvin Jones' Jazz Machine whined and whirred
And melted the candles.
Yes, yes and the music and the candles ricocheted
Across the room; yes, the music;
Yes, the music filled the room and leapt out the door
And paradiddled down the street
And yes into taxicabs and into sewers yes
Around corners and into alleys and up yes up,
Yes, and to the stars yes,
The universe was Jazz, yes,
The universe was Soul.

And I leapt out of Blues Alley and paradiddled
Into a taxicab where Elvin was playing
Yes and the meter flashed yes
And the windshield wipers were playing too
And Elvin Jones sat beside me and played,
And yes, I played with him.

TONE MATTERS

For a short time, I shared a studio with Michael Urbano, a well-known Bay Area drummer who has toured with a handful of internationally-renowned bands and recorded with many more. Michael is a super nice guy and a great player. His time and feel are impeccable. One day I came down to the studio a few minutes early for a lesson and found him practicing. I stood outside and listened for a few minutes before knocking on the door. I heard him playing the simplest rock beats and patterns you can imagine.

At one point, he kept hitting the floor tom over and over, slowly, one stroke at a time. I was struck by the apparent simplicity of what he was practicing, and I didn't understand it. Why would such an accomplished drummer be practicing something so apparently facile? I knocked on the door and went in, and we sat and chatted for a few minutes before my student arrived. When I asked him what he had been working on, he explained that he was about to go on tour with a prominent band and was replacing another very accomplished pro drummer. He told me he was "working on his tones." He had his headphones on and was listening to the sound of the drums on the band's recording. He was working on striking his floor tom to get the same tone he was hearing on the recording, or close to it. He told me he didn't want the band to feel like anything was different from the sound of the drums they were used to hearing. He was more concerned about the *sound* of his drums than trying to emulate the other drummer's parts note-for-note.

We went on to discuss the concept and importance of tone on the drums. He was a big believer in the critical importance of the quality of sound a drummer creates with every stroke on the drums and cymbals. He has even collected a huge number of drums from different musical eras to apply his desired tone concept to different studio recordings. I have no doubt this dedication to his tone quality is a significant part of why he is such an in-demand session player.

I was in my mid-twenties when I discovered the funk drummer Bernard Purdie. Though I'd heard his playing on Steely Dan and Aretha Franklin recordings, I didn't really know who he was, or why he was an important drummer. My first real experience digging deep into Purdie was from purchasing an album of his break beats meant for DJ's and hip hop producers. It was an album of solo drum grooves. And they were *phat*.

I vividly recall being astonished by the sound of his open hi-hat. It sounded like a spray of water on a sizzling hot skillet. It was powerful, hot, and crisp. I wondered how he could possibly get that sound out of his hats. And while there was certainly some engineering involved, I had no doubt that it was primarily the drummer who was responsible for the sound, and not a lot of production smoke and mirrors. So I wore that record out, and I tried for several weeks to get my hi-hat to sound like that. I had to completely break down my right-hand stroke and left foot pedal tension and rebuild them to work together differently. While I can't say that I was ever able to conjure that same mystical heat as Purdie could, I got pretty close. Of course, it's also true that the cymbals make a big difference, but I was more interested in what I could do with what I had than finding out which hats he played and running out to buy them. It made me much more aware of my hi-hat tone, and much better at manipulating my hi-hat tone to shape the sound of my grooves.

* * *

One of my high school students recently went off to visit a handful of colleges where he was considering applying. Intent on continuing to pursue his music education, he met with the jazz director and head drum instructor at one small college in Oregon to suss out the vibe of the program. He told me that he asked the drum instructor what was the most common shortcoming of people auditioning for him coming out of high school. A very astute question, I thought.

"That's easy," I said to him. "Time." "Actually," replied my student, "He said it was touch." After I considered it, it made sense. At the college level, most drummers should already have a decent sense of time. However, not all drummers play with a good musical touch. It occurred to me that I've heard several high school and college jazz band directors say this very thing to me—that at an audition, they can tell where a student is within 30 seconds, based on how they make the drums sound.

There is a way that drums sound different in different styles of music. To play hard rock for example, you need to hit the drums hard to really bring out the fundamental tone of the toms. And to play rock at all, you need to learn how to get a big, robust tone from your snare drum. (Kevin Army, who was the recording engineer on a number of Green Day albums, told me he asked drummer Tré Cool to hit the drums as hard as he could during their recording sessions.) To play jazz, on the other hand, you need to play with a much lighter touch, and draw the sound out of the cymbals and drums, almost like you're pulling a needle up through a piece of fabric. Sometimes this is referred to as "playing off" the drum instead of "playing into" the drum. (Erudite jazz drummer Peter Erskine describes this in one of his great instructional videos, and suggests the stick needs to vibrate freely in addition to the cymbal in order to get the best resonant tone.)

More advanced players do this instinctively and adapt their touch for the style of music they play. Greener players have a less refined touch and often play either too heavy-handed or too limply.

* * *

With the advent of electronic instruments, particularly the electric guitar in the 1930s–'40s and the synthesizer in the 1960s–'70s, the tones musicians created in their performances expanded to a whole new horizon. Until that time, songs were (comparatively) more characterized by their composition, i.e., the harmonic structure and melody.

However, once musicians started to reshape the sonic landscape with a nearly infinite palette of colors, you could make a case that the tone became just as much a part of the composition as the chords. Consider the opening riff to Jimi Hendrix's "Purple Haze." You can't even think of it without that distorted guitar sound. Or the grittiness of those early Kinks songs like "All Day and All of the Night," in which Dave Davies stuck some knitting needles in the driver of his amp to create the first "dirty" guitar sounds.

Many guitar players have crafted a definitive and instantly recognizable tone: Wes Montgomery, Bo Diddley, B.B. King, Jimmy Page, Stevie Ray Vaughan, Pat Metheny, John Scofield, Mark Knopfler, Robben Ford, and Bill Frisell, to name just a few. And certainly, there are many synth sounds that define the sound of certain pop bands of the 1980s (the Cars come to mind). While drummers aren't usually thought of as having distinct *tones*, the tonal qualities that drummers are able to draw out of the drums and cymbals matter just as much as their electric instrument counterparts. Indeed, you can trace the importance of drum tone back to the early jazz players, who, with notably fewer options available to them as far as different drumheads, sticks, cymbals, and drums, expertly crafted their tone with the resources available at the time. Drummers like Sid Catlett, Max Roach, Art Blakey, and "Philly Joe" Jones all had a distinctive sound on the drums, no less so than the modern era drummers like Steve Gadd, Hal Blaine, Jim Keltner, and JR Robinson; and you can't help but instantly recognize the sounds of Al Jackson, Keith Moon, Mitch Mitchell, and John Bonham, among many others.

TOUCH

Most of my students play with a distinct sound, a particular touch on the drums. I don't mean to say that they've evolved a distinctive personal voice—I mean they hit the drums the same way all the time (usually on the heavy side) because they haven't worked on developing their hands enough. If I were wearing a blindfold, I could probably tell them apart by each drummer's touch on the kit, particularly on the hi-hat and snare. I've never tried to do this, but I think I could get at least 50% right, if not more. I think this illustrates a number of things:

1. It makes clear how much of drum set playing is about your hands, how much work it takes to get your hands in good shape, and how challenging it is to develop dynamic control and a deft touch.

2. It demonstrates that most amateur drummers fall into hitting the drums in a certain way, and they don't work hard enough on breaking the mold they've set or learning to get different sounds out of the drums and cymbals.

3. It shows that I need to do a better job as a teacher helping my students work on their touch and awareness of their sound.

For the most part, touch is developed over time, the way a horn or a string player's tone matures over a period of years. It's fairly easy to recognize a beginning woodwind player by their tone. There's a hollowness to it, as opposed to the rich, full timbre you hear from an expert player. The same with a beginning string player, who tends to have a scratchy sound as they rake the bow across the strings. So it is with drummers. It takes years of practice to learn to manipulate the drumsticks so that eventually they feel like extensions of your hands, and you can draw the sounds out of the instrument with the goal of producing very specific timbres.

It's not a bad thing to be recognized for your sound. You just want it to be for a musical touch, and not a clumsy one.

TOOLS OF THE TRADE

The sounds you create on the drums and cymbals are of paramount importance to the overall sound of the music you play. Like a painter uses different paintbrushes for various visual and textural effects, so should the drummer use particular sticks, brushes, or mallets for the desired musical application.

I'm a Vic Firth guy. I think they are the best, most consistent quality drumsticks, and they have a staggering variety of options. (In full disclosure, I do have a Vic Firth endorsement, though I played Vic Firth long before I had any arrangement with them, and I stand behind their products regardless.)

My stick bag is full of a wide variety of sticks and implements for different playing applications. With all the different tip shapes, woods, weights, thicknesses, lacquers, and neck tapers, every stick will respond differently. Typically the difference will be more pronounced on the cymbals than the drums, but you can often hear a difference on the drums too, especially when it comes to weight and type of wood. (I once shared a high-profile gig with another drummer who had 10 pairs of the same stick in his bag. This made no sense to me.)

As a general rule, the bigger the stick, the bigger the sound. There are some sticks that are fat and light (typically maple, which I prefer), and some sticks that are thin and dense (hickory or oak). Generally, the thickness of the stick, the size of the tip, and the wood are good indicators of the volume it will produce.

If you are playing in an acoustic environment, like a coffee-house, or are playing jazz in a small group setting, you're going to want to play with a thin wood-tip stick. (For the record, I don't even own a pair of nylon-tip sticks. They're just way too ping-y and cold sounding for my taste.) A heavy rock environment warrants a heavier stick with a larger tip. In the end, it comes down to personal preference—you want to choose the right tool for the right job. If you want to cut through, you need a stick that will deliver a strong attack. If you want to be warm and mellow, you'll be hard pressed to sound that way playing a pair of 2Bs, or fat and heavy sticks. So choose the right stick for the right application.

For some years, each time I would end up in the drum shop, I would look to see if there were any new types of sticks, brushes, or hitting implements that had come out. If I ever found anything that piqued my curiosity, I would pick up a pair just to check them out and see if they created a sound that I wanted to have in my bag. Sometimes I'd find something I loved (like the Promark Broomsticks or the Vic Firth Tala Wands), and other times I'd find them to be a dud. The duds would always end up in my stick bag at my teaching studio. I always enjoy showing my students all the different types of implements there are to hit the drums and make different sounds.

I once saw the drummer Kenny Wollesen playing with jazz guitarist Bill Frisell, and I noticed that he had duct-taped an egg shaker to one of his sticks. I loved the sound, and right after the show, I went home to experiment with tape and egg shakers. I still have one in my bag today. (Painter's tape works best, as it won't leave a residue.) Since then I've seen a number of companies create a shaker attachment to a stick, with some even built into a hollow compartment in the stick.

The drum kit is just a collection of things you can hit, and there are no rules about how you have to hit them, or what you have to hit them with. Experiment with different types of sticks, including different woods, tip sizes, and shapes. Explore the sound of wire and plastic brushes, bundled rods, and various types of mallets. I even used to carry around a pair of squeaky-hammer toddler toys. (Eventually they ended up in the dud pile, but they were fun for a while.) Try playing with your hands; it'll help you learn to play with a lighter touch with your sticks.

* * *

For several summers, I worked at Cazadero Music Camp with a conga player named Edgardo Cambon, a top percussionist in the Bay Area. For the staff show event, he decided to put on a solo performance he called "It's not the drum." He found two wooden stools, set them up at the front of the stage with two close microphones, and proceeded to take a mesmerizing five-minute solo on them, playing them like a pair of congas.

The takeaway, on the surface at least, was that it's the drummer who makes the music, not the drum. Edgardo had explored the different timbral possibilities that the stools (which were remarkably resonant) had to offer. He lent his skill and musicality to different instruments than he normally played, and he made them sing.

A drummer can make an instrument out of just about anything: a suitcase, a trashcan, a teakettle, or a newspaper. Theatrical shows like STOMP and Blue Man Group are great examples of this. If you can hit it, it's a percussion instrument. Some found objects have more colorful musical possibilities, more voices, than others. It's the drummer's job to make those voices sing. After all, what are cymbals? They may cost an arm and a leg, but they're just metal plates that you hit to create a range of sounds.

When I was at Stuyvesant High School in New York City, each year a percussion quartet from Julliard would come to perform a private show in the band room for those of us in the symphonic band. They were exceptional musicians. After playing some marimba/xylophone pieces and snare duets, they would finish up with an improvised piece on a table full of ordinary household objects: cereal bowls, pieces of pipe, wooden boxes, and plastic cups. It was fantastically musical, and I was amazed by the sonic possibilities of all those household items.

I had a friend in college who was a professional drummer who played in a band with a second percussionist, who, at every show, would invite the audience to bring up anything they wanted for him to play as a percussion instrument. He would challenge the audience to bring him something he couldn't play. One time someone in the audience brought up a pair of 3-foot long salad-serving spoons. The guy played an epic solo on them, and earned a standing ovation.

The tools of the trade matter, but that doesn't mean you have to use the *traditional* tools of the trade. Find the implements to create the sounds you want, and add them to your toolbox. And have fun experimenting.

THE IMPORTANCE OF TUNING DRUMS

I can't tell you how many drummers I've come across, even many playing on gigs, who don't know the first thing about tuning drums— or even that they need to be tuned at all. No matter how expensive your drums are, they will not sound good if they are not tuned.

There are a number of devices on the market to help with tuning. Some measure tympanic pressure on the drumhead, others determine fundamental pitch, while others measure torque on the tension rods that hold the drumhead in place. Most of these devices help you get at least in the ballpark of being in tune.

I remember seeing the great fingerpicking guitarist Leo Kottke tune his guitar on stage using an electronic guitar tuner. "It's really just another opinion," he said, referring to the tuner, "when you've lost faith in your own." The same is true of these devices. By far, the best way to tune drums is by ear.

The problem is that most drummers haven't taken the time to develop their ear for the nuances of the pitch and "in-tuneness" of the drum and don't know what to listen for when they tune them. They also lack an understanding of how the two heads resonate together and how the tuning of the top and bottom heads affects the overall sound and response of the drum.

There are a number of excellent websites and resources for learning how to tune drums, so I won't go into detail here. But I will say that tuning your drums is of paramount importance. No matter how great you play, your drums won't sound good if they're not in tune.

CHOPS ARE JUST THE TOOLBOX

A master carpenter has the same tools in his toolbox as the apprentice, but knows how to use them much more skillfully. If you ask them both to craft a table, they will both be able to fashion one, and both creations will function as tables. But the master will create a thing that is technically superior and adds a refined aesthetic quality beyond its functionality.

Think of your chops as your toolbox. They are the means, not the end. I know that seems obvious, but there are unfortunately many musicians, especially drummers and guitar players, who don't understand this.

There is so much emphasis in the modern drumming culture on speed and complexity. Speedy drummers are lionized in most of the drumming magazines. There's even a World's Fastest Drummer contest, which is actually a competition to see how many single strokes a person can play on a drum pad in 60 seconds. It really has nothing at all to do with drumming or music.

I attended a clinic a few years ago presented by a well-known drum book author. His chops on the kit were very impressive. It was very valuable and I got a lot out of it. At the end of the clinic, he had the other two members of his trio come out, and they played a short set for about 20 minutes. I couldn't stand his playing. It wasn't musical, he didn't have a good time feel, and I thought his playing was uninspired.

Don't get caught up in the speed hype. Speed is important, and you need more or less of it depending on what style of music you play. Playing fast doesn't make you good. It just makes you fast.

THE TRAIN BEAT

I love a good train beat. A train beat is a drumbeat wherein the drummer plays a propulsive "chugga-CHUGga" 8th note pattern on the snare drum, augmented by the bass drum on downbeat and the hi-hat on the backbeat. The effect is the sound of a train chugging down the tracks. When the pocket is deep, there's nothing better.

In the mid-'90s, I played at a private party as a tribute for the great New Orleans pianist and producer Allen Toussaint. He was in town playing a brief stint at Yoshi's jazz club in Oakland, California. I was playing in a New Orleans R&B band at the time (Hot Links), and the bandleader was a devotee and scholar of New Orleans and roots music. Mr. Toussaint wasn't very well known outside of New Orleans at that point. He was gracious and affable, always a class act, as I would find out when he invited me to contact him down in New Orleans when I visited several years later.

We played a version of his studio classic "Hang Tough." He approached me on the break and complimented me on my pocket with it. "You really have to know how to swing those 8th notes just right. It's really easy to mess that up. You had a great feel with it," he told me. I beamed with pride. He even gave me an "official second-line handkerchief" with an imprint of his image on it as a token of his appreciation, which I still have.

In retrospect, it makes sense to me why he would have complimented me on that particular song, with that particular groove. The train beat is a simple groove, but a very sophisticated one. All the ingredients need to be refined and balanced just right in order for it to sound good. The bass drum needs to be present, but not overpowering. The hi-hat needs to be crisp and shut quickly to give it a snap on the backbeat. But the essence of the groove is in the way the snare part is played. The quiet notes need to be evenly weighted and the backbeat needs to come out just the right amount. Too much and it doesn't blend in the flow of the train, too little and there's not enough forward momentum. You can add selected accents to embellish it, but you need to be careful not to ornament too much. In short, it needs to feel just like a train chugging along with that propulsive chugga-CHUGga, chugga-CHUGga feeling. And you can't leave the snare ostinato or play any fills other than some subtle accent variations on the snare, or they stick out like hiccups in the groove—a monkey wrench in the train cogs.

The balance of the parts of the kit is key, as is the degree of swing, which is what Mr. Toussaint was referring to when he mentioned the 8th notes. It's difficult to maintain the right feeling of swing without fail, without even one note falling outside the pocket. It's a simple beat to construct, and a very challenging one to play at a high level. Sometimes it requires a further degree of coordinated independence, with the bass drum falling at times with the left hand, which for many amateur drummers can be a challenge. When the train beat is played expertly, and the bass falls right into the pocket with the drums, it is a force to reckon with, a chugging, grooving machine that invariably makes people want to *move*.

There are studio drummers in Nashville who make a living just playing this groove, which is very common in country music. It's also a mainstay of zydeco music, and can be played effectively with a lot of honky-tonk and boogie-woogie piano styles. It's worth noting that the left hand piano stylings of the early boogie-woogie piano players like Meade Lux Lewis, Jimmy Yancey, and "Pinetop" Smith are believed to have evolved from the pianists playing on and influenced by the sounds of actual trains, as they would be shuttled into logging camps in the piney woods of north Texas.

Some great train beat songs:

> "Hang Tough" (Allen Toussaint, from the album
> *Crescent City Gold*)
> "Lay Down Sally" (Eric Clapton)
> "Folsom Prison Blues" (Johnny Cash)

"Whirlaway" (Allen Toussaint)
"Got My Mojo Working" (Muddy Waters, et al.)
"Who Do You Love" (Bo Diddley)
"On the Road Again" (Willie Nelson)
"Last Train Home" (Pat Metheny)
"Two Step" (Dave Matthews Band)
"Traintime" (Cream)
"The Ballroom Blitz" (The Sweet)
"Thumbelina" (Pretenders)
"Radar Love" (Golden Earring)
"Walk on the Wild Side" (Lou Reed)*
"Honeycomb" (Jimmie Rodgers)

*This tune isn't a traditional train beat groove, but it has similar characteristics. Great groove in any case.

PLAYING BALLADS

As a young drummer just out of college, I found myself disliking playing ballads on jazz gigs. Booorrring. So slow, mostly textural playing with brushes, barely any punctuation...nothing to sink my teeth into. Horn players on the other hand seemed to love them. It was a break from the up-tempo stuff, and they got a chance to finally play with some nuance and emotion, lingering on tones and colors, instead of speeding through runs of notes and phrases.

At some point in my early thirties, I began to look at playing ballads in a whole new light. Or, more accurately, I began to *listen* to ballads differently. Instead of hearing them as saccharine and self-indulgent, I began to appreciate them as soulful and vulnerable. I'm not sure what caused the change in me. It could very well have been getting high and listening to "After the Rain" by John Coltrane, on the album *Impressions*.

Some of my favorite tunes ever written have been ballads. There are dozens of great versions of some of these tunes by different artists. Here are some that I love. Dig:

Song / Performer / Album

"Water from an Ancient Well" / Abdullah Ibrahim / *Water from an Ancient Well*

"My Foolish Heart" / Bill Evans / *Waltz for Debby*

"My One and Only Love" / John Coltrane and Johnny Hartman / *John Coltrane and Johnny Hartman*

"Body and Soul" / Coleman Hawkins / *Body and Soul*

"Something" / The Beatles / *Abbey Road*

"Across the Universe" / The Beatles / *Let It Be*

"'Round Midnight" / Thelonious Monk / *Quartet+Two at the Blackhawk*

"Peace" / Horace Silver / *Blowin' the Blues Away*

"Naima" / John Coltrane / *Giant Steps*

"Country" / Keith Jarrett / *My Song*

"Blue in Green" / Miles Davis / *Kind of Blue*

"Lover Man" / Billie Holiday / *Lover Man*

"Home" / Bonnie Raitt / *Sweet Forgiveness*

"Angel Eyes" / Wes Montgomery / *Brothers in Canada*

"I Want a Little Sugar in My Bowl" / Nina Simone / *The Very Best of Nina Simone*

"In Your Quiet Place" / Gary Burton & Keith Jarrett / *Gary Burton & Keith Jarrett*

"Mood Indigo" / Ella Fitzgerald / *Ella Fitzgerald Sings the Duke Ellington Songbook*

"Bird on a Wire" / k.d. lang / *Hymns of the 49th Parallel*

"A Child is Born" / Bill Evans / *Quintessence*

"God Bless the Child" / Billie Holiday / *God Bless the Child*

"Someone to Watch Over Me" / Stanley Turrentine / *Comin' Your Way*

The list goes on and on.

It's actually relatively easy for a drummer to ruin a ballad with too much flourish, too little dynamic support, bad time (hard to keep good time on the slow tempos!) or by just plain not listening. I know, because I used to do it all the time. Now I enjoy playing ballads. It's a chance to shift gears and paint more impressionistically with brushes and mallets, to use colors and sounds that I don't get to use in other contexts. With a slow and open feel, what you play is more exposed. The subtlety you employ can be appreciated, every nuance apparent. And if you're playing with a good vocalist, horn player, pianist, or guitarist, and the band is feeling it together, you can really take the music to another plane.

NAME THAT TUNE

There will always be jazz musicians who are stuck in the decades gone by. And while I don't begrudge anyone their love of playing the music of say, the 1930s, I find it much more compelling to listen to modern renditions of old music that have something interesting, new, or creative to offer. As for rock covers, I love to hear an artist take some unexplored facet of the original and dig deeper, shine a light on a dimension of the tune that demonstrates a fresh and creative interpretation of it, or maybe even reinvent it.

For instance, Devo's version of "(I Can't Get No) Satisfaction" is a fantastic example of a new and different conceptual take on the original by the Rolling Stones. It deconstructs the anthemic, driving rock song into a quirky, almost spasmodic reggae-infused groove, and makes you consider the lyrics in a slightly different way. You still feel the protest and cynicism from the bold original lyrics, but the reimagined groove, with its hypnotic, angular repetition—along with the halting, at times stuttering delivery of the vocals by Mark Mothersbaugh—suggests more disquieting agitation or anxiety, rather than the gritty complaint of the Stones version.

Or take Led Zeppelin's brilliant version of Joan Baez's "Babe I'm Gonna Leave You," another great example of a band taking a song and digging deeper into its psyche. Baez's version—itself a cover of the lesser-known original by Anne Bredon—is dark and chilling, with a Flamenco-style acoustic guitar rapidly arpeggiating the chords under her soaring, haunting vibrato. It sets the monochromatic soundscape for the lyrics, which describe the visceral pain of a lover wanting to stay but feeling compelled to leave. The song works as a snapshot, almost like a black and white photograph distilling the human experience into a moment of emotion.

The Zeppelin version, on the other hand, is more like a color motion picture. The arrangement moves back and forth between Robert Plant's soulful, wailing vocal over a simple acoustic guitar (paying homage to the Baez version), to the full band riffing on a heavy syncopated rhythm, increasing in intensity each time they hit it, until it bursts open with a driving, anthemic chorus. Jimmy Page's serpentine guitar solos wrap around Page's visceral, desperate vocals, adding texture and dimension to the slower sections. The overall effect really underscores the existential dichotomy expressed in the song, amplifying the intensity of the emotional angst in the lyrics.

Similarly, Sam Beam (Iron & Wine) does a beautifully stark rendition of The Postal Service indie hit, "Such Great Heights." Stripped down from the pulsating techno TPS arrangement, Sam sings it accompanied only by his acoustic guitar and some dulcet vocal harmonies on all but the first verse. It reveals the pathos in the lyrics that the original never fully does, and it has a vulnerability and earnestness that is not present in the original version.

Sometimes artists hear something in a song that they can imagine in a different context, and they take an existing song and tell a different tale with it. That's what I like to hear in a rock cover: the old made new. Occasionally, the cover version is so much more compelling than the original that it becomes a hit song in and of itself, whereas the original never got much commercial traction. Sometimes people don't realize that familiar popular songs are actually cover versions of an original.

Some of my favorite rock covers *(original artist in parentheses)*:

Talking Heads—"Take Me to the River" *(Al Green)*
Ike & Tina Turner—"Proud Mary"
   (Creedence Clearwater Revival)
Aretha Franklin—"Respect" *(Otis Redding)*
The Byrds—"Mr. Tambourine Man" *(Bob Dylan)*
Elvis Costello—*"(What's so Funny 'bout)*
   Peace Love and Understanding" *(Nick Lowe)*
Joe Cocker—"With a Little Help from My Friends"
   (The Beatles)
The Clash—"I Fought the Law" *(Sonny Curtis)*
The English Beat—"The Tears of a Clown"
   (Smokey Robinson)
Jeff Buckley—"Hallelujah" *(Leonard Cohen)*
Sinéad O'Connor—"Nothing Compares 2 U" *(Prince)**
White Stripes—"Jolene" *(Dolly Parton)*
Johnny Cash—"Hurt" *(Nine Inch Nails)*
Iron & Wine—"Such Great Heights"
   (The Postal Service)
Santana—"Black Magic Woman" *(Peter Green)*
Cake—"I Will Survive" *(Gloria Gaynor)*
k.d. lang—"Bird on a Wire" *(Leonard Cohen)*
Beck—"Leopard-Skin Pill-box Hat" *(Bob Dylan)*
Nirvana—"Lake of Fire" *(Meat Puppets)*
Lyn Collins & James Brown—"Do Your Thing"
   (Isaac Hayes)
Janis Joplin—"Me and Bobby McGee"
   (Kris Kristofferson)
The Rolling Stones—"Not Fade Away" *(Buddy Holly)*

Mark Ronson ft. Amy Winehouse—"Valerie"
  (The Zutons)
Jimi Hendrix—"All Along the Watchtower" *(Bob Dylan)*
Jimi Hendrix—"Wild Thing" *(The Troggs)*
Alison Krauss & Robert Plant—"Killing the Blues"
  (Rowland Salley)
Bonnie Raitt—"Angel from Montgomery" *(John Prine)*
Otis Redding—"Try a Little Tenderness"
  (Ray Noble Orchestra)
Devo—"(I Can't Get No) Satisfaction"
  (The Rolling Stones)
Led Zeppelin—"Babe I'm Gonna Leave You"
  (Anne Bredon)

*Prince actually released a studio version of this song on an album under a different band called The Family. It was not released as a single, and gained little recognition. Sinéad O'Connor's rendition was the first to gain wide exposure.

In the past 30 years or so, jazz musicians have also taken popular rock and pop songs and re-harmonized their chord structures, or altered their rhythmic basis, dramatically changing the concept from the original. In fact, jazz musicians have been doing that with popular songs from well before rock and roll ever came on the scene (for instance, with popular show tunes by the Gershwin brothers and Cole Porter). As a musician who grew up listening to the popular music of the '60s, '70s, '80s and beyond, I have a soft spot for jazz versions of rock tunes from those eras.

Some of my favorite jazz covers of rock tunes:

Herbie Hancock—"Mercy Street" *(Peter Gabriel)*
John Scofield—"What'd I Say" *(Ray Charles)*
Bill Frisell—"Live to Tell" *(Madonna)*
Brad Mehldau—"Blackbird" *(The Beatles)*
Brad Mehldau—"Knives Out" *(Radiohead)*

The Bad Plus—"Everybody Wants to Rule the World"
(Tears for Fears)
The Bad Plus—"Life on Mars" *(David Bowie)*
Joshua Redman—"Tears in Heaven" *(Eric Clapton)*
Medeski Martin & Wood—"Hey Joe" *(Jimi Hendrix)*
Casandra Wilson—"Last Train to Clarksville"
(The Monkees)
SFJAZZ Collective—"Superstition" *(Stevie Wonder)*

THE MOST RECORDED DRUMMERS

As jazz music waned from popularity and R&B and rock 'n' roll took their places in the mainstream in the 1950s, drumming became more about groove and feel than about punctuation and soloing. Of course, the great jazz drummers had incredible time feel too, but the window for creativity was much smaller in a groove-based context.

Though in almost all styles a drummer's job is to propel the music, the R&B or rock gig is in some fundamental ways a different animal than the jazz session. Jazz drummers can come to the canvas with a much wider range of colors and ideas, and can create them on the fly to fit the music as it moves from bar to bar. Groove drummers for the most part need to pick a color and stick with it. Their job is to pick just the perfect part for larger chunks of the music (a verse, a chorus, or even an entire song) and make it feel just right. Jazz drumming is sort of like a Jackson Pollock painting: it's a constant rendering of impressions within an overarching structure that is challenging for some people to perceive. Rock drumming has more repetitiveness, with more obvious structure.

The early rock 'n' roll and R&B drummers were actually jazz players who understood that the music was changing, and applied their accomplished musicianship and prescient instincts to this new form of music. They played rock drums with a jazz drummer's sensibility. Their fills functioned perfectly in their simplicity and tastefulness and their grooves were irresistibly danceable and upbeat. They knew how and when to play on the front side of the beat and when to lay back. And, they often had the luxury of playing with the same studio rhythm section members for a number of years. Nothing like familiarity to breed groove.

Earl Palmer, Pistol Pete Allen, Al Jackson, Benny Benjamin, Steve Gadd, Hal Blaine, JR Robinson...these guys together have played on more hit records than just about every other drummer in history combined. The later generation guys, Gadd, Blaine and Robinson, took groove playing to the next level. Like musical chameleons, they were able to adapt parts for a wide range of sub-styles of rock and pop music, and with well-honed instincts, come up with just the right part every time.

All these drummers, and others like them, shared something rare and special: that perfect blend of facility, instincts, time and feel.

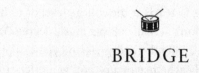

BRIDGE

Drumming in the World

MUSIC AS A CAREER

As a freshman at the University of Michigan, I spent some time seriously considering transferring to music school back in New York City. I'd gotten the application to the Manhattan School of Music jazz program and even filled it out. But I never sent it. I decided a liberal arts degree (I ended up majoring in literature) was a good thing to have, and that I could always go back to music school later if I decided that's what I wanted to do. I also thought that if I chose to pursue a career playing drums, I didn't necessarily need a degree in music to do it.

Unless you're looking to teach at the college level or to become a serious composer, you don't actually *need* a music degree. You can teach in high school with a liberal arts degree, and you can play and write songs professionally whether or not you've gotten a degree in anything. The main thing you get from going to music school is *immersion*. You get at least four years of living and breathing music, playing, practicing, learning theory and piano, music history...and meeting other musicians. You get many ensemble playing opportunities, private lessons with great teachers, and a lot of performance experience.

In short, I think music school as an experience makes you a better player, and certainly a very well-rounded musician. But you can also become a better player by pursuing your own path of study and practice, just like many jazz musicians did before they offered degrees in jazz performance. And when you graduate, you enter the pool of musicians who have also been honing their craft, and you're competing with experienced professionals for the same gigs a lot of the time.

When my students tell me they want to pursue a career as a professional drummer, I encourage them to think about why, and I ask them what that looks like to them when they imagine it. Many of them have unrealistic notions about it, and I talk to them about my experience and those of my peers, some of whom went to music school. I can usually tell (though admittedly, I don't think my high school drum teacher or band director would have suspected that I would have chosen this path)—there are some kids who are just so passionate about it, so hungry to learn, they *can't not* pursue it. It's what they're driven to do, and it's clear that this is the full expression of their vocational purpose and passion in life. These kids will become professionals regardless of their experience with me, and I feel honored to work with them and help them along their journey.

For just about everyone else, I generally recommend that they go to college and get a bachelor's degree in some other field, assuming college is part of their trajectory. I encourage them to pursue music as a secondary endeavor. I remind them that if they work really hard, they can get as good as their music school counterparts and still have a degree to fall back on in case the music path doesn't work out.

Ninety-nine-point-nine percent of the time, making a living as a musician is not at all glamorous. Most musicians I know, even some at the top of the Bay Area scene, piece together a living playing gigs and often teaching lessons, with some portion of both not fulfilling to them. Since playing cover songs in a casuals band often pays so much more than playing creative original music, they end up subsidizing their art with a handful of better-paying gigs that may not be as satisfying.

There are a number of avenues available to the modern professional to make a living playing music: you can play union gigs in touring musical theater pit bands, or work the community theater circuit (which pays much less); you can play in wedding or corporate bands (which tend to pay much better); or in an original rock band (which tends to pay almost nothing). Generally, jazz gigs pay a little more since the venues are paying for atmosphere, whereas rock clubs are paying bands a percentage of the door based on their draw. It's not until you get into the larger venues (meaning you're more commercially successful) that you can start earning a reasonable amount of money for your time. Even then, it's not necessarily a huge payday, and those gigs are few and far between unless you're on tour with a well-known band. Tours don't last forever (unless you're the Rolling Stones), and often you're lucky to break even financially when you finish.

There are other paths, like writing songs in the hope a famous musician will pick one up, scoring for films or TV, writing jingles, licensing your music for commercial use, remixing, or being a session musician. There aren't as many of these jobs available as there used to be, and most of the time it's extremely difficult to break into the ranks of journeyman players. So, I tell my students to consider getting a day job so that they won't need to rely on the meager living of a working musician. That way, music can be something they play for fun and soul satisfaction, and they can be as selective as they like about who they play with and what gigs they take.

In the 1990s, I started seeing a "Real musicians have day jobs" bumper sticker all over the place. At the time, I remember thinking that real musicians were the ones like me who *didn't* have day jobs. The problem with both points of view is the word "real." There is nothing more or less real about musicians who play for a living versus those who don't need to rely on the income from their gigs to get by. Should the professional who mails in his performance because he's not happy playing on a gig be held in higher esteem than the musician who has a regular job but makes sacrifices to play gigs on the weekends that he loves to play? It's a meaningless comparison in the end. What matters is that you do what you love.

One of my friends is an intellectual property lawyer at a prestigious law firm. His clients are some of the biggest names in modern music. He told me one time that he had written the contracts for the touring band of a very famous musician. The drummer on that tour is a household name, probably one of the top 25 drummers on the planet. I was curious, and asked my friend how much the drummer was making on the tour. "I can't tell you that," he said, "but I can tell you that I'm glad I'm a lawyer and not a drummer." Here was a drummer at the absolute top of his craft, and he was only making an average wage to go on tour for a year with a famous musician who had a "brand." By average wage, I'm talking about less than six figures for a yearlong tour. For anyone else at the top of the world in his or her field, that would be a low wage indeed.

If you're getting into music for money and fame, you're almost assured of a rude awakening. To survive as a musician, you need to love it. In the end, the most meaningful thing is that you do what you love. If you can do it and live comfortably, all the better. And if you can be one of the rare people who make a lot of money at it, more power to you. Personally, I'd rather do what I love and live with less, than work at some soul-crushing job and make more money.

Most artists would say, I think, that they pursue their art because they have to. It takes a lot of sacrifices to follow one's passion. I have great respect for my fellow artists and the sacrifices they make to pursue their art.

ENDORSEMENTS

When I was an aspiring drummer in my early twenties, I thought that if I could just get an endorsement, I would really be accomplished and successful. I have several endorsements now, and I can tell you they really don't change your life a lot. You could say that they burnish your professional reputation, and there is some merit to that. And while it's nice to save some money drum gear, how many drum kits and cymbals can you really buy? How many pairs of sticks do you go through in a year? Not enough for the savings to add up to very much. More important than the savings are the relationships I've built with some of the great people at Brooks Drums, Aquarian Drumheads, Sabian Cymbals, Prologix Percussion, Vic Firth Drumsticks, and Protection Racket Cases. It's nice to know that the people there are there for me when I need gear, and will support my equipment needs with repairs, advice, careful selection, and personal attention.

I want to address the legion of drummers out there who are fixated on getting endorsements: r emember that these companies need to get something in return for supporting you. If you don't have much to offer besides wanting a feather in your cap and some discounted gear (it's almost never free, contrary to popular belief), why would they spend their very precious time catering to your needs? Remember, these are relationships with people who, in turn, work for larger companies, and you've got to have something substantive to offer if you want to get something meaningful in return.

Endorsements are not supposed to be for everybody, and you can disavow yourself of the fantasy that a drumstick endorsement means you get free drumsticks for the rest of your life. Unless you are already famous (even the top endorsers have a limit on how many sticks they receive), in which case you didn't really need free drumsticks anyway. It just doesn't work that way. If you work hard to make a name for yourself, play in front of large audiences on a regular basis, or are engaged as an educator with influence in your school or community, you may have something to offer, and you can send a polite and unassuming inquiry, preferably with the recommendation of an existing endorser. It's really important that you should believe in and use the product. Remember, it's called an "endorsement," and not just because the company is endorsing you. You are expected to endorse them too.

DON'T BELIEVE PEOPLE WHO TELL YOU WHAT YOU CAN'T DO

On a trip across Europe in 2000, my girlfriend and I decided to travel east and spend a few nights in Prague. It was the most foreign feeling of the places we visited, and it wasn't difficult to discern remnants of Soviet-era repression woven into the fabric of the culture there. Eager as we were to experience as much as we could of what the city had to offer, one night we ventured out looking for live music. After navigating our way through labyrinthine streets, we descended a staircase into a subterranean jazz club, where a young jazz-fusion band was playing.

We ended up talking to the musicians and hanging out with them after the show. They told us about another club nearby where the "who's who" of Czech jazz players were having a jam session. Turned out there was some conference that week in Prague that all the top jazz educators and players were attending, and many of the faculty were playing at a session at this club. We went and sat down and had a drink…and were blown away. You could have heard these cats at any of the top jazz festivals around the world and they would not have been out of place.

I've heard ignorant people assert that only Americans can really play jazz, since it was originally an American art form. I've read musicians opine in interviews that only Jamaicans can really play reggae, and that women can't really swing. That is 100% bullshit. Music doesn't know where you come from; it doesn't recognize race, gender, age, or anything that makes us different from one another. If you spend your 10,000 hours or so listening, studying, and living and breathing any style of music, you will become a force to reckon with.

When I was in college and considering pursuing a drumming career, one of my dorm-mates told me he didn't think I had what it took to be a professional drummer. Don't ever let anyone tell you what you can't do. Listen to yourself. If you love it, do it. Believe in yourself and trust your vision. Become the fullest expression of your passion. In the end that is the most important thing.

MO'FONE

One of the bands I play in, Mo'Fone, is a trio of just two saxophones and drums. The group came together serendipitously. I had a trio gig with a bass player and a sax player (Jim Peterson) at a local brewpub back in 2003. As the drummer, I'm almost always the first musician to arrive, since it takes extra time to load in and set up. So I set up my kit in a corner of the bar and waited for the other musicians to show up. Sax players will often arrive only 5–10 minutes before downbeat on these local gigs, since they can be ready to go in just a couple of minutes, and there is no sound check.

The gig is about to start, and it's just me and Jim. No bass player. We wait a few extra minutes, and decide to just start playing as a duo. It's a bar gig, so it's not a huge deal, but as a professional, it's embarrassing not to have the group performing as promised. (I've got worse stories of musicians showing up late or not at all at much higher-profile gigs.) So we have some fun in the spare duo context. But after the first set with a lot of drum solos, Jim and I discuss whether we know any other players who live nearby who might want to come out and just jam with us. Thing is, the only other player we know who lives nearby is another saxophonist. So I give Larry De La Cruz a call, and he's not gigging that night and would be happy to come by and play with us. Two saxes and drums. It ended up being one of my most favorite, and path-changing, gigs.

With such non-traditional instrumentation, we were free of the prescribed roles typically associated with each of our instruments. With no harmonic context for the sax solos, Larry and Jim traded off playing bass lines. Emancipated from the restrictions of leaving space for bass, piano, or guitar, I filled up more space with both rhythmic and melodic support. I used toms and tones more than usual, and was able to punctuate with cymbal punches and an active kick drum to help shape the bottom end. In short, we were venturing into conceptual territory that none of us had explored before. It was totally liberating, and we each felt like we played with terrific creativity that night. It was really fun.

So much fun in fact, that we decided to do it again. And again. And again. Over time, we grew more comfortable with our different roles in the stripped-down context, and we began to explore the compositional possibilities our unique instrumentation afforded us. Where at first we just played jazz standards and occasional rock/pop covers, soon we started picking tunes that lent themselves to our chord-less trio. Jim quickly switched to baritone sax to fill out the bottom, and Larry stayed on alto, though they occasionally stretched out onto flute, clarinet, and bass clarinet. As we got more comfortable, we started to sound fuller and fuller. We noticed that our ears would often fill in what we would have thought would be missing. Jim started to jump back and forth between bass lines and harmony, and he and I would lock in on hits and grooves, giving each song its own unique arrangement. We recorded our first album in 2005, and it received voluminous critical acclaim.

Over time, we began to think about writing our own music for the trio, and on our second and third albums we took advantage of the knowledge we'd gained from years of playing together without further accompaniment to compose music specifically for the group. You can hear a tremendous amount of evolution in the concept of the band over the course of three albums, which span 13 years. We also invited some special guests to join us on the albums—horns only, of course (and on one tune, didgeridoo)—including such luminaries as Dann Zinn, Dave Ellis, Danny Bittker, and Kirk Joseph from the Dirty Dozen Brass Band, who added colors and layers without changing the fundamental sound of the group. We ended up being invited to perform twice at the Monterey Jazz Festival, and several times as part of the San Francisco Jazz Festival, among others. We've also won several awards.

On a couple of occasions early in our tenure playing together, we had gigs where one of the sax players couldn't make it. We tried subbing out the gig to a couple of capable players, but each time the result was a disappointment. Despite rehearsing and having charts to read and arrangements to follow, the band never really jelled. We meandered through tunes with little cohesion and lacked the usual creative spark and sense of adventure that we had grown accustomed to on every gig. It made us aware of how much we had evolved as a trio, and how much our sound depended upon us as individuals and the chemistry we had with one another. Now if we get a gig where one of us can't make it, we turn it down. Mo'Fone is Mo'Fone.

At one of our gigs at the renowned SFJAZZ Center, we were fortunate enough to be performing on the same night as the legendary New Orleans musician Dr. John, a hero of mine ever since I started digging his music in college. (Check out *Dr. John's Gumbo*, a masterful tribute to the music of New Orleans, and one of my all-time favorite albums.) The SFJAZZ Center has two stages: the larger auditorium, which seats about 900, and a smaller performance venue, which holds about 100. Since both bands were performing at the same time, we ended up having dinner with Dr. John's band in the dining area designated for the musicians upstairs. Though we were excited to hang with his band, Dr. John stayed in his private dressing room preparing for the show. We were disappointed to miss having a chance to interact with him.

As it got close to downbeat, his band finished up dinner first and left to get ready. A few minutes later, we got cleaned up and exited the dining area to begin the walk downstairs to the stage. As we turned the corner in the hallway, we came upon Dr. John and his band huddled together in a circle, arms draped around one another's shoulders. "Oh, sorry," I said, reflexively. "We didn't mean to interrupt." Dr. John turned to look at us. He was wearing a purple suit and matching beret, a chest full of Mardi Gras beads, and two long, feathered necklaces. His right hand was resting on a cane for support. I could feel the magnanimity of his presence immediately. "Come on in!" he implored in his unmistakable raspy drawl. The musicians opened up the circle to let us in, and we joined in the huddle with the rest of his band. We leaned our heads forward.

"Let Spirit bless dis gig," he said, "And make dis de best gig we done ever played." I closed my eyes, taking in the moment, and the intention. We stood for another few seconds, then joined in a chorus of "Yeah!" and "Yeah you right!" with the rest of the musicians. I floated down the stairs to the stage, beaming. We played our asses off that night. It helped that we had gotten some medicine from The Doctor.

SURROUNDING YOURSELF WITH PLAYERS WHO HELP YOU GROW

There's a reason John Coltrane and Elvin Jones played together for such a long time. Likewise, Clifford Brown and Max Roach, Miles Davis and Tony Williams, Elton John with Nigel Olsson, Bruce Springsteen with Max Weinberg, Billy Joel with Liberty DeVitto, and so many more. As in romantic relationships, it's important to surround yourself with people who help you grow. And so it happens that in music, when people find they work well with one another, they will often continue to work together, touring and recording, for many years.

There's a comfort in being so familiar with the way another musician plays, to know their tendencies and tastes. Like on a good basketball team, it feels like there's some level of telepathy happening, where you know where people will be and what they'll do before they do it.

It takes time to develop that familiarity and trust, and when musicians develop it with one another, they'll often try to hold onto it as long as they can. And why wouldn't they? It's not easy to come by, and every time you play with new musicians, it adds unknowns into the mix. Certainly that can be refreshing at times, and new personalities can help move the music to new and positive places. But when the groove is happening with players you know and trust musically and personally, there's nothing better.

I'm a big believer in surrounding yourself with musicians who are simpatico. We work so hard to get to where we are; it's nice to share the experience with people you enjoy playing with and whom you feel are on the same page. This also explains the longevity of bands like the Rolling Stones, U2, Green Day, and other longstanding groups—and why drummers jump at the chance to sub for these bands, or replace the drummer when there's a rare opening. It's not just that it's a high profile or lucrative gig, it's that they get to play in a band that is already highly refined and functioning at a very high level, and be a part of something special.

* * *

Back in the early '90s, I had a gig in San Francisco every other Saturday at a local brewpub in North Beach. The gig hardly paid anything, I think it was $100 for the trio, but you could pass the hat during breaks and end up with another couple of hundred in tips from tourists. They fed us too (they'd better for a paltry $100), and all told it was a fun gig, despite the abysmal dearth of parking in the North Beach area.

I had gotten the gig by playing with some other groups there, and made friends with the bartender, who was also the talent buyer. He gave me two Saturdays per month, and I was welcome to bring in whatever project I wanted.

For most of the next two years, I decided to treat the gig like my own musical laboratory. I played with a different trio just about every time, sometimes using the same players in different configurations. We played mostly standards, though I also brought in charts of tunes I liked, pop and rock stuff, and we'd play the occasional funk, reggae or second-line tune to mix things up. I had numerous piano and bass trios, guitar and bass trios, horn with bass, horn with guitar, and occasionally odd groupings like two guitars, and even two saxophones. Sometimes we'd have guests come and sit in or sing a few tunes. I took advantage of the opportunity to connect with a couple dozen really phenomenal musicians, including some very bright lights in the Bay Area jazz scene.

As you might imagine, playing with a different group of unrehearsed musicians every gig, the results were mixed. Some nights we really found something special, and everybody knew it, even the tourists knocking back their fourth and fifth beers. Other nights it felt more meandering and unfocused, and the groove wasn't as happening. Not all of the best nights happened with the most talented or experienced players. In fact, I found that the technical proficiency of the musicians (and mind you, everybody was a very capable professional player) actually had little impact on the outcome of how good the music felt. My favorite nights were ones when I played with other musicians who I clicked with; ones who had similar concepts of rhythmic punctuation and flow, ones who were responsive and supportive.

Looking back, I am extremely fortunate to have had this opportunity in my early twenties to meet and play with so many great musicians, and luckier still to learn so much about music and about my own playing from the experience. I can't remember why I stopped playing the gig. I do remember toward the end feeling less and less satisfied with playing unrehearsed music. I wanted to play with just my favorite three or four musical companions, to rehearse and get tighter, to come up with creative arrangements that made the music feel more interesting and cohesive; I wanted to evolve more with the musicians with whom I felt most comfortable, most myself. From that experience, I ended up putting together my own quartet (the J. Steinkoler Quartet), making an album, and gigging with the same musicians for a number of years.

ONE SIZE DOESN'T FIT ALL

As a drummer, I've performed with bands of all sizes, up to 50-piece concert bands. I've played in duos with guitarists, pianists, saxophonists, violinists, vocalists, drummers, beatboxers, and poets. Beyond the standard jazz and dance bands, I've played in trio and quartet configurations with dozens of combinations of instruments, including a wide range of winds, brass, strings, voice, and percussion...and with a handbell ensemble, a solo clowning act, and a person playing on a globe (world beat)...even with a group playing the zippers of their sweatshirts.

I always enjoy playing in different musical situations and with new instruments or in unusual combinations. I find that every different setting offers the challenge of figuring out how much sonic space to take up and how interactively to play. My role might be the dynamic engine of a power rock trio, the propulsive finesse of the jazz trio, or the light finger-playing color/texture with an avant-garde poet. Every situation offers differing degrees of freedom and responsibility. I love that.

I listen to all kinds of music and to groups of all different sizes. Some of my favorites are smaller groups, especially trios, where you can hear the interaction of the musicians more clearly and the drummer has more room to roam. One of my all-time favorites is Jack DeJohnette with Keith Jarrett and Gary Peacock. Each musician's contributions are on par with the others', and the group works as one, improvising through often loosely structured song forms that offer plenty of open space for adventurous harmonic and rhythmic exploration. Check out "Endless" off of the live album *Changeless*, recorded in 1987.

WHY EVERY DRUMMER SHOULD LEARN TO READ MUSIC

Many times, students will come to me for lessons and insist that they don't want to—or need to—learn to read music. Though it is true that there are many professional drummers in the world who can't read music (for what it's worth, there are even some famous piano players who can't either), I tell my students that those drummers are at a disadvantage if they can't read.

There are many types of gigs that require reading: jazz ensembles, pit orchestras for Broadway shows, high school productions, any orchestral or classical music, even some rock gigs, and, most importantly, plenty of recording sessions, from singer songwriters to soundtrack music for movies. The list goes on: I've even been on other, more unique gigs that required reading, including working for a company that put on musical corporate team-building skits at company retreats; a gig with a poet, and playing along with spoken word. If you can't read, you can't take these gigs.

Still, you might say, "I don't want to play any of those kinds of gigs. I just want to play in a rock band." To which I would reply that there is an even more important reason to learn to read than getting gigs: you can become your own teacher.

If you can read, you can work through instructional books, transcriptions, and other educational materials. You can learn from lead sheets and scores. You can teach yourself new styles, new patterns, and absorb new concepts more efficiently. You can recognize and understand the relationship of different concepts to one another and open up whole new worlds. And you can communicate with other musicians in the universal language of written music.

ON BEING PREPARED

A few years ago, I was offered an opportunity to audition for a well-known touring rock band. I thought about it for a few days before deciding I didn't want to try out. I imagined how I would feel if I got the gig, and realized that I didn't really like the music all that much. Better someone else should get the gig who really wanted it, *I thought. I mentioned this opportunity to a friend of mine, another pro drummer and teacher whose playing I know well. His eyes nearly popped out of his head.* "They're one of my all-time favorite bands!" *he exclaimed. I put him in touch with my contact, and he got an audition. Several weeks later I heard that he'd gotten the gig, and ended up touring with the band across Europe for a summer until their original drummer decided to return to the band. I was happy for him.*

A few months later, we were catching up over lunch and talking about his experience at the audition and the subsequent tour, and he shared with me his process for getting ready for it. He told me that his plan going in was to do everything he could to be as prepared as he could possibly be. He knew that there were several other accomplished players auditioning for the band, and he wanted to do everything in his power to stand out. He told me he wanted the band to feel like they couldn't possibly not choose him.

He learned every song on the audition set list so that he could play them all by ear. By the time the audition came around, he knew the arrangements cold. He also prepared several additional songs that were not on the list, in case they wanted to play some other tunes or offered him a chance to suggest one from one of their other albums. He then hired a professional bass player friend to practice rehearsing the songs with him, so he could practice playing the songs live, with some subtle elasticity that the recordings couldn't provide. He recorded his playing in Pro Tools, then overlapped the tracks on top of the band's original recordings to see how things lined up, and checked to see if there were any parts he tended to rush or drag. He went into the audition confident, knowing that he was well prepared. As to whether he would get the gig, he told me that all he could do was to assert influence over what was within his power to control. If he got the gig, he'd be thrilled. If he didn't, at least he could feel good about having given it his best shot, and could walk away with no doubts about having prepared as much as he could.

He arrived on time, was pleasant, easy to work with, and enthusiastic about the music (it was one of his favorite bands, after all), and nailed it. They called him the next day to let him know he'd gotten the gig. He was ecstatic that his hard work had paid off. They were supposed to play a local show the following week before embarking for the tour and would be rehearsing with him until then.

The following day, he got a very contrite call from the band's musical director (MD) apologizing profusely for what was about to transpire. Apparently, that morning the band had gotten a call from a very famous drummer who said he was available for the tour and interested in the gig. The MD was apologetic, but they felt that they just couldn't turn down the opportunity to play with this highly regarded drummer, whose popularity might also help sell tickets to their shows. Though he was devastated, my friend was polite, and thanked the MD for the opportunity.

The following week, my friend got yet another call from the band. Apparently, the band had played the local warm-up show with the famous drummer. He'd come in not really knowing the tunes, and flubbed several of the arrangements; obviously he had not done his homework and did not prepare adequately for the gig. Perhaps he felt that his skill and talent alone would count for enough to carry the show. The band realized their mistake and asked my friend if he would join them on tour after all. Though it was a roller coaster to get there, he went on tour and had a great experience.

I love this story for so many reasons. For starters, my friend had the discipline to prepare as thoroughly as possible. (Incidentally, I had another very advanced student who also auditioned for the band, and did not prepare as thoroughly. Needless to say, she didn't get the gig.) I told him I thought his idea to overlay his tracks on top of the band's CD was brilliant. He was digging deep, and it was clear how much he wanted it. Plus, in spite of his arduous preparation, he had a great attitude: though he really wanted the gig, he wasn't so emotionally attached to the result. Instead he channeled his desire into his preparation. He discovered things about his playing, and he learned a whole new set of tunes with various feels by emulating another drummer's time feel. He handled the entire process with such grace, humility, and professionalism. His dedication and work ethic ended up carrying

the day over a more accomplished drummer, who relied
on his reputation instead of putting in the time that was
necessary—one whose ego likely got the best of him.

Eventually the band's original drummer returned to
the group, and my friend parted ways with the band.
But while he was with them, he had a great experience
playing for huge festival and stadium crowds, earned a
cymbal endorsement, and learned a lot. He even made a
bit of money, and he had fun.

ON AUDITIONING

Many of my students have to grapple with the daunting experience of going through an audition for their high school jazz band. Others try out for local amateur rock bands, and some even make it to the professional level and get to audition for well-known touring and recording bands.

Typically, the average high school jazz band audition is very brief, maybe 5–7 minutes at most. You'll be asked to demonstrate facility with a handful of different grooves and feels, including swing (medium and up-tempo), bossa nova, Latin, funk, and possibly a waltz or a samba. You'll be asked to trade fours or take a solo, and you'll need to sightread a chart. Sometimes there will be a prepared piece required as well. In my experience, it's often the reading that dooms the audition. Most teenagers can competently swing and play the grooves. (If you can't, go practice!) A good number can at least trade fours competently. Consider, however, that band directors are looking for a drummer who they don't need to worry about or handhold. They've got their plate full with intonation and articulation issues with 15–20 horn players. The last thing they want to worry about is a drummer who can't read and set up figures—or worse, one who struggles to keep time.

Many high school band directors can tell within roughly 30 seconds where a student is developmentally. This is another reason why it's so important to make a strong first impression as soon as you start playing. Play with confidence. Even if you're nervous, don't play meekly. Play like you deserve the spot.

When trying out for an established band, remember that as talented or famous as people may be, they are just people, with humble beginnings like everyone else. Be easy to work with. Don't try to steer things too strongly in your direction, don't monopolize rehearsal time by talking about yourself or your parts, and don't put your ego on display.

Remember to *listen*. Listen to the music, but also listen to the banter and dig the vibe of the session. If the guys are loose and like to joke around a lot, you can be at ease and meet them at that place. If the vibe is super focused and the musicians don't want to waste time getting down to business, then take that cue and get to work.

Be on time; I can't stress that enough. Being late to a rehearsal or a gig is a vibe killer, and you may find yourself digging yourself out of a hole for a while to regain people's trust and respect. Obviously, shit happens and things come up, and a good reason is a good reason. If you're going to be late, apologize, and get to work as quickly as you can—but don't be late.

If you're at the audition, the implication is that you are good enough to get the gig. Trust the skills that have gotten you there. Be confident, but humble. Nobody likes to play with a cocky musician. Show enthusiasm for the music. If you have to manufacture that, you really shouldn't be auditioning for the gig. Be sure the gig is really what you want: to play *that music*, and to work closely with *those people*. Consider that an audition is just as much about sussing out potential relationships as it is about the music. It's important to feel comfortable working together. You are auditioning them just as much as they are auditioning you.

Be flexible. Offer input if appropriate; don't insist on things going a certain way. Be open to trying different parts and taking suggestions. Always try things out to see how they feel. If they told you to prepare a set of tunes, then ask you to play one you didn't prepare, go with the flow. They might just want to hear how good your instincts are, or see how you work under pressure. You can mention you didn't work on it, but are up for trying anything.

Have your gear together. If you need to bring your own kit, make sure everything is in working order. Don't come in and apologize for the sound of worn out heads or a broken hi-hat clutch. Think of the audition like a gig—make sure your gear is good to go, and have backups in case things break.

Ask them how the auditions have gone thus far—not to gauge your chances, but to break the ice and connect—you know how grueling and challenging a long day of auditions can be. Thank them afterward, and tell them you appreciated the opportunity to play with them and look forward to hearing from them.

One time, the New Orleans R&B band I was playing in was auditioning a new bass player. We probably spent about a half hour each with six or seven guys one afternoon, all of whom had solid résumés and came highly recommended. The last guy to show up started off by asking us how the auditions had gone so far that day, and asked how *we* were feeling. "Long day, I'm sure," he said. It was an empathetic gesture, and it wasn't lost on me. I appreciated that he wasn't just thinking about himself. Turned out he was also an empathetic player, and his feel was far better than anybody else's we auditioned that day. He got the gig.

In short, be professional, and be cool. If you are, you'll easily set yourself apart from at least 50% of the other drummers who auditioned for the gig.

SETBACKS...AND RECOVERIES

As a music teacher, you're different parts instructor, mentor, therapist, mechanic, advisor, motivator, and role model. You get to see people at their best—and sometimes at their most vulnerable—and once in a while, both at the same time.

Most of my teenage students have gone on to participate in their high school jazz programs. In the San Francisco Bay Area, the large population density means that most of these programs are moderately to highly competitive. Usually there are two drummer spots in each ensemble. To get into the top groups, the drummers need to be superlative players.

By 15 years old, many drummers have already been practicing for several years and have dedicated themselves to their musical development at the expense of other pursuits. They have a lot at stake in their ascension through the ranks of their fellow high school drummers and into the coveted ensemble spots.

I celebrate with my students when they pass the audition and make it into these bands. I remind them about all the hard work they put in, and I tell them they really deserve the credit for making it to where they are. They earned their achievement through their dedication and should be proud of their accomplishment, while at the same time recognizing the work that still lies ahead. When they don't get into the bands, I remind them that sometimes it takes repeated attempts to make it; that if it were easy it wouldn't mean as much, and that we can use the temporary setback as motivation for working harder as we move forward.

I try to be as supportive as I can be. I've personally experienced both results of the audition. I imagine there aren't too many drummers who haven't. I know how painful a setback it can be when you don't get in, especially for teenagers who are already enduring tremendous social, academic, and parental pressures, all while trying to make sense of who they are and how they fit into the world.

Sometimes my students can be devastated. I had one student whose friends all made it into the ensemble, while he got left behind for the second year in a row in the practice band. He was so distraught that he quit the program, and soon after quit playing drums, despite my efforts to help him acknowledge how much he had accomplished and how strong a player he was.

Other times, the failure serves as a motivating experience. Instead of feeling rejected and depressed, another student who didn't make it into the jazz program as a freshman channeled his energy into doubling down on his practicing. He got in the next year and made it into the ensemble as a senior. He went off to music school and is playing at a professional level.

You just never know how students will handle the experience of rejection. For some, it ends up being a fork in the road—they turn away from music and the pain they associated with their experience. For others, rejection is nothing but motivation to help them work harder to succeed. And then, every so often, I get a student who is somewhere in-between, who could go either way. I think it's with those kinds of students that a teacher can have the most meaningful impact. If there is already a strong trust developed, a teacher's support and guidance can help those students overcome their self-pity and help motivate them to move forward and continue to grow.

I sometimes share my own stories of rejection with my students. It helps them to see that even a successful professional can experience rejection and setbacks along the way—and that those experiences can be part of the journey, and not the end of it. I even tell them that when I was 12 years old, I quit playing drums for a couple of years, letting my drum kit collect dust in my room while I pursued other interests. Then in high school I was inspired to start playing again, as there were more opportunities to play in bands. But most of all, it was because I found a great teacher.

SOLO

For Musicians of All Stripes

FINDING YOUR VOICE...

I have a student whose father, an accomplished pianist, told me when he came to my one of my funk gigs that he could tell immediately as he entered the club that it was I who was playing the drums. I took it as a compliment. Many great drummers are instantly recognizable by their sound. John Bonham, Keith Moon, Mitch Mitchell, Stewart Copeland, and of course the jazz greats: Max Roach, Elvin Jones, Tony Williams, Buddy Rich, to name a few of the most famous...each of them crafted a sound and had a touch and feel that defined their playing.

Anyone can develop a distinct way of expressing themselves on their instrument. My ultimate goal as a teacher is to help each student work toward finding his or her own voice as a player. This is a process that can take many years and extend well beyond the time a student spends under my tutelage. I didn't feel that I found my voice as a drummer until I was in my thirties, and I feel like it has continued to evolve since then. To be sure, some people can find it earlier, but it takes a lot of work to evolve to the point where you feel like you have a distinct, personal sound and way of playing your instrument...*and* have something meaningful to say with it.

Some musicians spend so much time trying to emulate other musicians that they never find their own voice. Even the great Miles Davis admitted in his autobiography that in the beginning, he was trying to sound like Dizzy Gillespie. He'd practice and practice, but would return from gigs feeling distraught and defeated that he couldn't play with the range and speed that Dizzy played. At some point, he realized that that wasn't who he was. He needed to find his authentic self, to figure out who *Miles* was and what *he* had to say.

This whole concept may sound a little odd to some, since it can be difficult, at least for the layperson, to pin one artist down to sounding a particular way. Furthermore, artists evolve, and different drummers may sound different with different bands. After all, part of what makes Keith Moon so recognizable is the sound of the Who. Likewise, with John Bonham and Led Zeppelin. But as you listen to drummers more and more, you can start to hear certain qualities in their playing that go beyond the sound of their drums and the distinctness of their band. You can discern a concept in their phrasing and articulation, a unique way of hearing things and contributing musical ideas. And you can identify their preferred vocabulary.

We are all sponges—we absorb, and we filter. We listen to music, take lessons, go to live shows, and practice. We are influenced by the time we live in, the way we listen to music, our nature and our nurture. All these things make up who we are as musical individuals. It makes sense then that each of us has a unique way of playing and thinking about music, based on the particular synthesis of our various influences, and the idiosyncrasies we each bring to the table.

...AND STAYING TRUE TO YOURSELF

At a Mike Clark clinic I went to, he talked about playing the song "Actual Proof" with Herbie Hancock on the album *Thrust*. His wildly creative approach on that tune made it a seminal recording, and it is widely regarded as one of the nastiest linear funk grooves of all time. It didn't start out that way. As Mike tells it, at first the producer wanted something much more straightforward. After several takes trying to play what the producer wanted, he asked to try it once the way he wanted to play it, the way he heard it in his mind. It ended up being the keeper take.

Learn to advocate for your vision. Be flexible, and try things on for size—usually producers are there because they have good instincts, and they can help you develop your ear for what sounds good—but in the end, you have to live with yourself and with what you play. So make sure you believe in what you're playing, and stay true to your musical vision as much as possible.

TRYING IT ON FOR SIZE

I once had a very talented student who played in his high school jazz band. He was well into some advanced material, transcribing Art Blakey solos and playing musically at a high level. As tasteful as his playing was, he hadn't yet learned to play with presence. *His playing was always just a little weak sounding, not tentative exactly, but not assertive either. He played as though he lacked confidence, even though he was a very capable player.*

I went to see him perform with his high school ensemble. His ideas were great, but his playing lacked power and conviction and failed to really drive the band. At his next lesson, I told him as much, and we worked on some mental exercises for playing more assertively and with more confidence. Over the next few weeks, he began to come out of his musical shell a little bit.

Around this time, his band attended an adjudicated jazz festival, where bands from the region go to play in front of a panel of judges who critique them and offer advice on how to improve. During the instructional clinic, where a judge worked with the band directly and ran them through a rehearsal, my student was singled out for playing too loudly and assertively. He came home from this experience and reverted to playing even more meekly than he had before. I wasn't at the festival, but it was difficult for me to imagine a scenario where he played too strong. When I inquired whether he had played out more than usual for the judges, he said he played like he usually did.

Not all advice is good advice. For starters, it's important to recognize who's giving it. If it's coming from a known person, whose musical opinion you respect, it's probably worth heeding. If it's coming from someone you don't know, you can take it with a grain of salt, but there still might be some value in it. I've gotten good advice from strangers, and bad advice from people I know. Take with you what resonates and makes sense, and let the rest go.

Sometimes others can offer valuable perspective on our playing that we aren't aware of. It could be related to timing, a repetition of ideas or lack of creativity, or issues with tempo or dynamics. One thing is for sure: the tape doesn't lie. Listen back to your playing on recording or video, and most of your issues will become clear very quickly. Or better still, listen or watch with your private teacher who is already familiar with your playing. With an experienced pair of ears listening attentively, you can get right down to what you really need to work on.

Teachers are guides. Nobody has the last word on your playing, except you. Some teachers will try to mold you in their image, instead of encouraging you to find your own voice. Be wary of teachers who do this. A teacher should help you establish a strong foundation of skills and help you clarify and achieve your goals. They should teach you how to practice effectively and impart their wisdom from having done this for (usually much) longer than you have. That doesn't mean your perceptions and experiences aren't valid. Your observations may not have the wisdom from years of experience, but they may be enlightened just the same.

WHAT I LEARNED FROM THE MAINTENANCE WORKERS AT THE SOUTH STREET SEAPORT
(and also from James Brown)

When I was 17 years old, my friends in my high school jazz combo and I decided to play a handful of gigs on the street in New York City, busking for tips. It was a great way for us to practice, and to practice performing. Sometimes we made some decent money, although I almost always had to spend whatever I made on the two taxi rides back and forth to my parents' apartment with my drums, since we didn't own a car. We played in Central Park, on 42nd Street, in front of the New York Public Library, and at tourist destinations like the South Street Seaport. From one of these gigs, we actually secured a gig at the Village Gate playing as the house band in front of an audience of 400 people, including Paul Shaffer, the musical director from the *David Letterman Show* band. It was a talent showcase of street performers a producer had found all over the City, and it was the highlight of my high school career.

Occasionally, we'd get a few people taking a break from their busy lives to listen for a minute or two to a group of high school jazz musicians do their best to swing and strive to say something. Usually, they'd smile and give us a thumbs-up and drop a dollar in the saxophone case we'd put out in front of the band. Sometimes they'd stay and chat with us in-between tunes, asking us questions about music, or our age. On rare occasions, like the one in Central Park, we had a large group of people sitting on the grassy area around us, digging some jazz on a sunny afternoon. For the most part, people would just walk on by, and not pay us much heed.

One Sunday we were playing on the sidewalk just outside of the South Street Seaport, going through our repertoire of jazz standards. We'd made about $20 in tips. Despite the large number of people passing by, nobody was paying us much attention. Just as we were thinking about packing it up, a group of four maintenance workers got off their shift and strolled by our combo. They stopped to listen for a good while, chatting amongst themselves and digging the music for several tunes.

After about 15 minutes, they approached us, smiling with enthusiasm. They told us they really dug the music, and that it was a shame nobody was stopping to listen. One of them said he was going to do something about it. "Gimme a beat!" he exclaimed, pointing at me. I started to play a funky beat. His three friends started clapping their hands, while the first one started shouting out to the passersby that something was going on right here. Like a practiced hype man, he implored the slowly assembling crowd to put their hands together and "dig what was happening right here and right now!"

Before we knew it—and to our utter astonishment—there was an audience of 40 or so people assembled in a semi-circle around the band. The bass player and guitarist had picked up the groove, and the saxophonist started blowing over the vamp. Our new front man kept feeding the crowd, riling them up with enthusiasm for the music, clapping on the backbeat and pumping them up in general about nothing in particular. And of course, once there was a sizable crowd, more and more people stopped to see what was going on. It grew exponentially. Within a few minutes, there were easily a hundred people grooving on the scene.

The four of us in our combo stole smiling glances at each other, giddy with the attention we were getting, and at the same time almost embarrassed for it. We weren't used to that big an audience. I think we also recognized that it was the showmanship and charisma of this dynamic and generous maintenance-worker-turned-concert-producer that had brought the crowd.

During these few minutes, while our new front man worked the gig like a seasoned pro, one of the other guys took off his hat and started walking through the throng, shoving the upturned cap in front of everyone and asking for them to "give it up for the band."

I think we made $200 in the span of 15 minutes. As there was nothing more to the show after this brief escapade of crowd-fluffing, the guys generously handed us the cash, wished us the best, and left us to continue playing to the assembled 100+ people.

Without the dynamic, engaging entertainer working the spotlight, the crowd slowly dispersed. Five minutes later, we were playing the same tune to about three or four people.

"Holy shit," I said to the bass player. "What the fuck just happened??" He looked back at me and shook his head, unable to put words to what had just transpired. The sax player understood. "That," he said, turning to look at us, "was entertainment."

And so it was. It was a great lesson in what engages people, what makes an audience feel like there's something to *engage in*. Sometimes it's not enough for musicians to just play (OK, often it can be, at the higher levels of jazz or classical music for example); sometimes there's got to be something more. *People want to be entertained*. Every good showperson understands this. You've got to work the crowd, feed the energy, and show them how to have a good time by having one yourself on stage.

I remember seeing Buckwheat Zydeco playing for a solid hour without breaks at the New Orleans Jazz & Heritage Festival. About 45 minutes of it was call-and-response with the audience, with exhortations like James Brown would make on stage: "Somebody scream!" "Lemme hear ya say yeah!" "Put your hands together!" and so on. These guys are pros, and they know how to put on a show for a large crowd. Yes, you definitely have to bring the music (and James Brown, one of the greatest entertainers of all time, also had one of the tightest bands of all time). You also have to *bring the show*.

We nodded in gratitude to those maintenance workers at the South Street Seaport as they walked away, while we continued to play. Little did they know they weren't just making us a couple hundred bucks, but teaching us a lesson that would last a lifetime.

CONTEXT MATTERS

Like many musicians, I have had the experience of playing at a crowded venue as "background music." I've played at many corporate parties and cocktail events where the music is really just for atmosphere. For the most part, these gigs pay very well, and most musicians I know are happy to get the call for a "casual," where they know they'll make some decent bread. Sometimes that's just fine, and the musicians have their own semi-private fun while the people in attendance mostly ignore the music. Occasionally, you'll get one or two people who dig the caliber of music that's being played and will spend most of their time listening to the band. Most musicians know that these types of gigs are great for making money, and not for making music to be appreciated as art.

If you think about it, it's kind of a funny thing. I can't think of any other artistic medium where its purveyors are hired as a commodity not to be appreciated as art, but to provide a general ambiance for some event. You don't see accomplished painters or sculptors or poets being hired for weddings or corporate events. Balloon animal makers maybe (but that's really more of a craft), or magicians perhaps—though even magicians walking around performing tricks are appreciated for their craft and showmanship, and engage people directly with their art form.

The same ensemble playing at a wedding making a couple of thousand dollars can perform at a club the next night and make next to nothing. Same level of musicianship, same professionalism, same artistry, but for a fraction of the price. Is there somehow less intrinsic value in the performance context?

On the one hand, at weddings and high-end events, there is an expectation of everything costing a lot. The event *means* more to those putting it on, and they're willing to pay to make it special. The going rate among wedding/corporate bands is naturally much higher than that of bands performing at clubs. And the service providers (band, photographer, caterer) need to manage the client, catering to their needs and timetable, and are hired to make sure the event runs professionally and smoothly. That's worth something. But now we're looking at this as a professional service being provided. What of art? Isn't it art that people want to surround themselves with for their special event to help make it more meaningful?

The best gigs, of course, are the ones where musicians make their music as art and it is appreciated as such, and they also get paid well, like gigs at regional festivals and prestigious venues. My most memorable Bay Area gigs have usually been at places like Yoshi's in Oakland, the Freight & Salvage in Berkeley, the SFJAZZ Center in San Francisco, Sweetwater in Marin, or at larger regional festivals. The audience is there for the music, and you can feel their appreciation for your art. The artists are treated (usually) as creative royalty, and the audience is there first and foremost to dig the music.

Once you reach a certain point in the arc of your career, those are pretty much the only gigs you play. Until that time, if it ever comes, a gig can offer a musician three possible benefits: It can be lucrative; it can be good for one's career (as in playing at a prestigious venue or with a well-known band); or it can be playing creative music one is passionate about. Most musicians I know believe that a gig has to have at least one of those things going for it to be worthwhile; if it has two, it's a very desirable gig; and if it has all three, that's about the best you can ask for.

* * *

I used to wonder whether people would recognize the genius and artistry of say, Miles Davis or John Coltrane, if they heard them playing on the street, or in some unfamiliar context where they didn't expect to hear great musicians playing. Turns out I don't have to wonder anymore. In 2007, Gene Weingarten, a reporter for *The Washington Post*, had the brilliant idea to run a social experiment to find out the very same thing. He asked a world-renown classical violinist, Joshua Bell, if he would be willing to play for an hour or so in a subway station entryway at the Metro in Washington, D.C.

This was a violinist who had earned the most superlative accolades from classical music critics and performs to sold-out audiences at the most prestigious venues for hundreds of dollars per ticket. For the experiment, he played on a Stradivarius violin costing several million dollars, and he performed what are considered some of the most difficult and beautiful classical pieces ever written for violin. Out of 1,000 people who passed by during the 45 minutes he played, seven stopped to listen (including one person who actually recognized Joshua Bell). He made $32 in tips.

In 2016, the rock band U2 did a similar kind of stunt with Jimmy Fallon from *The Late Show* on a New York City subway platform. The band was dressed up in disguises, and drummer Larry Mullen, Jr. was playing on a kit assembled from buckets. In the video, which was clearly edited (and was meant more as a fun stunt than a social experiment), it appears that the band plays a song and generates little interest from the onlookers waiting on the platform. A few people seem to be noticing and listening, but the band isn't getting much attention. At a certain point, Jimmy Fallon exclaims, "OK, this isn't working!" and pulls off his disguise, and the rest of the band follows suit. The crowd quickly recognizes the band and soon a larger crowd gathers around them and starts taking pictures in disbelief. My hunch is that unless an onlooker had recognized the band, they would not have generated much more interest than the average band that plays on a subway platform or out on the sidewalk busking for tips.

Context matters. It can determine whether you make $50, $500, or even $50,000 for playing the same music, with the same passion and artistry. It can determine whether or not people listen to your performance, and whether they are held in rapt attention, applauding after every song, or ignore you entirely. It can determine not just whether people connect with you and your music, but whether they even allow themselves the opportunity to. In short, the context of a performance is a crucial factor in determining how music (and I think art in general) is perceived, or even whether it's perceived at all. Some people in the Joshua Bell experiment, upon being interviewed after they left the station, didn't even recall hearing any music in the Metro station entryway.

I used to get frustrated playing music at crowded bars or pubs where most people wouldn't bother to listen. Now I try not to take it personally, and instead I put it in the perspective of the context in which I'm playing, the way I imagine Joshua Bell had to when 1,000 people passed him by in the Metro station and ignored him. Because even when a tree falls in a forest with no one around to hear it, it still makes a sound.

DISSONANCE IS IN THE EAR OF THE BEHOLDER

Among other things, jazz pianist and composer Thelonious Monk introduced a radical harmonic concept into jazz. He was one of the first piano players to embrace what had up to that point been considered "dissonance." Before Monk, it was generally implicitly understood that playing a minor second (any note and the next closest note to it at the same time) was a no-no (although, ironically, it is the tension between these two notes on the 3rd and 7th steps of the scale—though not played at the same time—that had been used to great effect by early blues singers). The tension created was too dissonant, and by most accounts sounded "wrong." Monk embraced the minor 2nd, and made it palatable, even sonorous.

His angular melodic twists and harmonic concepts changed jazz forever. No longer were certain intervals or chord colors taboo to play. On the contrary, they were *interesting*, and offered contrast and richness to the harmonic tapestry of the sonic landscape. It was as if he introduced an entirely new dimension to jazz, a whole new color palette. He was also a terrifically inventive rhythmic player, and his melodies and solos featured displaced rhythmic motifs and syncopations that hitherto had not been commonly played.

Pioneer that he was, his music wasn't really appreciated by many people other than his fellow musicians until decades after his death. My producer friend at Blue Note Records (who later became the chief archivist for the Sony/Columbia Jazz Division) told me that in one year during the early '90s, they sold more Thelonious Monk records than they had during his entire lifetime.

Monk had a tremendous influence on all jazz musicians who came after him, whether they know it or not. One such musician is Kenny Werner, an acclaimed New York-based jazz pianist who traveled around in the 1990s teaching seminars on music and improvisation. At one of his clinics I attended, he talked about how dissonance is really a value judgment we listeners place on what we hear; that there is no inherent *goodness* or *badness* to sounds, just different colors and textures, different emotions that are elicited. To drive his point home, he proceeded to play the jazz standard "All the Things You Are" in two keys simultaneously, one with each hand. The keys were a half step apart. By all measures, this should have sounded terrible, and "wrong": dissonant, uncomfortable, and full of tension. He prefaced his playing by telling us exactly what he was going to do, and suggested that it would sound beautiful, if we would just listen without judgment and open our minds to embrace the unusual color of it. And in all honesty, it sounded beautiful to me, and I saw many heads nodding in agreement. Expectation matters. And dissonance is in the ear of the beholder.

INSIDE/OUTSIDE

Thank goodness there are people in the world who will challenge our beliefs. Without them, we might end up stuck in the same narrow-minded way of thinking forever.

I used to believe that in order to play something "outside" (in the jazz world, this loosely means to play inventive and creative harmonies outside of the established or conventional way of thinking), you first had to learn to play "inside." Meaning that to be creative and play something new and different, you first had to learn to play the conventional way, to know what you were departing from. I once raised this very point at a clinic with the avant-garde saxophonist Steve Coleman. "Man, that is 100% bullshit," he said. I was shocked. I was indignant. I was 22.

He was right. There are no rules about what you need to learn. It may be a really good idea to learn diatonic harmony and scales, and how scales relate to chord changes in order to improvise. Understanding music theory can help explain how compositions are put together, give you a deeper appreciation of what you're listening to and playing, and help you listen more critically. Knowledge of the history of music can offer context and insight into music that might otherwise feel inaccessible. However, you don't need to know any of that in order to be creative or inventive. It just *helps* to know it.

I've known sax players who are artful and adventurous improvisers, but who don't necessarily understand the music theory behind their solos. I've played with bass players who have a deep pocket, but who have scant understanding of even the most basic music theory. I've worked with drum students who can play sophisticated and musical jazz solos, but haven't yet studied Max Roach, Buddy Rich, Roy Haynes, or Jack DeJohnette.

I love listening to the masters and learning music theory. I much prefer to have some kind of map to navigate the constantly changing topography of the vast world of musical expression, though I can respect that not everybody chooses to explore that way. Some just like to venture out into the creative wilderness and see what happens. In the course of *Songs in the Key of Life* (also a great Stevie Wonder album), there is no required syllabus—only suggested reading.

JAZZ TUNES ARE VEHICLES

In the early '90s, I went to see tenor saxophonist Joe Henderson play with Al Foster on drums and George Mraz on bass at Kimball's East in Emeryville, California. It was one of the most memorable shows I've ever seen.

To my surprise at the time, they played only standards. Not just a range of familiar and lesser-known tunes, but a short list of only the most frequently-played standards you'd find in the *Real Book*. "Take the 'A' Train," "Body and Soul," and a dozen or more others. And they killed it.

Around that time, I had been playing a lot of jazz gigs and was growing tired of jazz standards. I had begun to feel like there wasn't much more to say with these tunes, which had been played so often by so many people (including myself), they had become hackneyed and lifeless. And then I heard Joe Henderson and his trio breathe vitality into these melodies and solo over these familiar chord progressions with refreshing creativity.

It was a stunning wake up call. It taught me that as chord progressions, jazz tunes are just vehicles for improvisation. Though the chord progressions may be familiar or common, there really is no end to how creatively and expressively you can play over them. Likewise, the melodies of these songs are catchy and often beautiful lyrical statements, which is what made them popular songs to begin with. What's more, jazz musicians can take such liberties with these melodies that they can make each performance uniquely compelling.

Every chance to play music is an opportunity for *transcendence*.

And those tunes, despite their prevalence, are perfect vehicles in which to explore uncharted territory. After all, it's not the car you drive, but where you go with it that matters.

WITH GREAT CHOPS COMES GREAT RESPONSIBILITY
(or, Nobody Expects the Chopsy Imposition)

One of the best shows I've ever seen was at the SFJAZZ Center in San Francisco, one of the finest venues for live jazz in the country. It was a trio without a drum set player: Béla Fleck on banjo, Zakir Hussain on tabla, and Edgar Meyer on upright bass. Three musicians at the very top of the heap on their respective instruments, each a world-class virtuoso in his own right, with deep roots in a variety of idioms and experience crossing over into other styles.

There were times when there were an astounding number of notes going by in every bar, and there were times when they each barely played. The music lived and breathed, expanded and contracted. At every moment, there was close listening and musical cooperation among the three musicians. Throughout the night, their playing demonstrated a restless search for connected moments, full of inventive phrases, memorable passages, and evocative moods. For all their collective chops, not once did I feel like their facility did not serve the music.

I find this to be true of the best musicians: everything they do serves the music. They are in utter control of their instruments, and their technique is clearly in service to their ideas and creativity. John Coltrane, Charlie Parker, Elvin Jones, Max Roach, Jack DeJohnette, Brian Blade, Herbie Hancock, Chick Corea, Bill Evans, Jimi Hendrix, Stevie Ray Vaughan, Chris Thile, Leo Kottke, Itzhak Perlman, Yo-Yo Ma...the list goes on, and cuts across all styles of music. The primary focus is the final result, the big picture, and every ounce of musicianship and skill is put to that end. When you have great chops, it's pretty easy to put them on display. But great musicians also have great instincts. They know what *not* to play just as much as they know what to play.

* * *

In 1999, I was fortunate enough to visit the Van Gogh Museum in Amsterdam and see some of his masterpieces up close for the first time. I sauntered through the gallery from painting to painting, marveling at his bold use of color and his expressive brushwork. Then, from the corner of my eye, I saw "The Sower" (Sower with Setting Sun, 1888) from across the room. I stopped suddenly, rooted in place…then felt as if a magnetic force was pulling me toward it. At first it was the magnificent, explosive sun that piqued my interest from afar. As I stood and stared at the painting for a half hour, I discovered richer and deeper layers of color, dozens of shades of blues and yellows and browns; many hundreds of brushstrokes, each seemingly applied with intention. It was as if the artist knew all along how each swipe of his brush would ultimately fit into the whole.

When you look at a great painting, you are overcome with a general feeling; there is an experience of taking in the whole in all its power and magnificence, and it can be evocative and stirring. The longer you look at it, the more you go on a journey of discovery and appreciation. And as you get up close, you can start to see some of the meticulous attention to detail and appreciate the intention of every stroke serving the whole picture. So it is with great music.

A WHOLE GREATER THAN THE SUM OF ITS PARTS

In the world of sports, you often hear talk about team chemistry, about how intangibles are a crucial part of success. Any general manager or coach of a team can tell you that all it takes is one player to undermine the group dynamic and foul up what could otherwise be a very cohesive unit. In sports, music, business, politics—just about any aspect of life—whenever you have a group of people working together toward a common goal, you inevitably have to deal with egos. As soon as any one ego becomes too large, or if you have an individual who cannot or will not work cooperatively with the group, you compromise the ability of the group to achieve its goals.

Good team chemistry, while a crucial ingredient for success, by itself is not enough. You still need skill, leadership, talent, dedication, and insight. There are times when, with the right balance of personalities, talent, input, and hard work, a group can achieve things greater than the sum of its parts.

I have witnessed this in the context of BandWorks on many occasions. I've heard amateur bands sound accomplished, well beyond their collective years of experience. In these cases, each musician plays a part that they can play well, not reaching for something too sophisticated or beyond their ability. It may be a different version from what's being played on the original recording, but it's a part they can own and play with confidence. The drummer keeps time and the singer sings on pitch, in a comfortable key. The arrangements are tight from many repetitions in rehearsal, and the band plays like they're having fun. The individual musicianship may not be very high, but the band plays well together as a unit.

Usually, after running the band through a song, I'll have a lot of feedback to offer: the tempo picked up, the guitar player missed the bridge transition, the bass player played the notes too staccato or detached. But sometimes, when everything clicks, and the band plays a song that sounds greater than the sum of its parts, I just nod my head and smile.

Conversely, I've seen concerts where the individual musicians were very highly skilled—world class, even—and the show fell flat. I once attended a show at the prestigious Paramount Theater in Oakland. It was billed as a tribute to Antonio Carlos Jobim, and the star-studded band was full of luminaries on every single instrument, some of the biggest names in jazz. It was a huge band: vibes, guitar, two piano players, bass, drums, and several horn players. Since it was a tribute show, I suppose the producers just invited a whole stable of players to come and contribute, figuring all those big names would sell tickets, which they did. Unlike a tribute concert where each famous musician gets up and plays a tune or two with the band, in this case, the entire band played the whole time. And it was not happening—the individual musicians themselves were indisputably great—but the band as a whole did not sound rehearsed, and it never felt like they were on the same page. With so many chording instruments, there was far too much "stepping on toes" in the rhythm section, and the musicians often seemed at cross-purposes with one another. With the chaos of the alternating comping instruments, soloists were not well supported and it never felt like the band jelled the entire night.

The bigger the group, the more moving pieces there are, and the more important rehearsing and direction become. While any of those musicians could have performed with a trio or

quartet and put on a fabulous show, all together, they made
kind of a mess. I doubt that any of them would have disagreed.

It was a good reminder that success comes from talent-
ed people working in harmony together as a whole, focused
together on a common purpose, and working to each indi-
vidual's strengths. And, that without direction and good
communication, even the most talented individuals striving
toward the same goal can work at cross-purposes to one
another, with less than desirable results.

Under the best of circumstances, bands vibe and feel the
energy of the show together and play authentically, without
artifice, from their collective souls. I believe any band can do
this, from the beginner to the world-class professional. When
they do, the resulting whole is always greater than the sum of
its parts.

QUICK IMPRESSIONS

I once read an interview with guitarist Pat Metheny about hearing
saxophonist Joshua Redman play for the first time. He said something to the effect that he could tell Josh was a special player from the
first few notes he heard. At the time, I wondered, *is it really possible*
to tell that quickly that someone is special, or has something worth-
while to say?

When I hear new students play for the first time, or when I go
out to hear a new local band, I must admit that I tend to make judg-
ments very quickly. Not that an artist can't grow on me or disappoint
me the more I hear them, but I find that I am able to get a fairly
good sense of musicianship and artistic integrity in just a few bars.
For many musicians, when they've been playing long enough, they

can assess the quality of what they're hearing fairly swiftly. Just like those producers like Berry Gordy of Motown Records fame, who could tell you within four bars if the song was going to be a hit or not—and somehow, they were always right!

Even when a musician is playing something relatively simple, you can still hear the control, the tone, the *intention*, immediately. It's especially evident when you see them play live. Body language, even how a musician holds an instrument, can tell you a lot. Really experienced players demonstrate a command, as if the instrument is there to do the bidding of its master. With greener musicians, the instrument often appears overwhelming to them, as if they are daunted by the potential complexities of it—their fingers imprisoned by a cage of strings and frets, clumsily maneuvering around the bottom of the neck; a drummer practically diminished by the physical stature of the drums, unable to bring forth any range of color, or stuck with a severely limited vocabulary. More experienced musicians exude a confidence when they play, a trust in their facility bred by years of practice. You can hear it, and see it, immediately.

CODA

Life Lessons

LEMONADE

I once played a wedding in Carmel, California with my dance band. It was a three-hour drive, a long way to go for a casual and drive back the same night. But the pay was good, and the clients were friends of friends, so we took the gig. The event was at a beautiful winery, set among picturesque rolling hills. The weather was a perfect 70 degrees. We set up inside of the barn, which was really more of a ballroom inside a rustic facade. The dance music was supposed to start right after dinner, around 8 pm. We were also told in no uncertain terms that the venue had a strict cutoff of amplified music at 10 pm. We planned to play one long two-hour set, straight through, to give the clients what they paid for.

We had dinner along with the wedding guests, then waited for the toasts to finish before we started playing. And we waited...and waited. We were ready to go at 8 pm, but the toasts kept dragging on. We stood around the bandstand ready to hop up on stage as soon as we got the signal. Every time we thought we were ready to go, someone else would stand up to make another toast. And another. By the time the toasts were done, it was 9:45 pm. The bride and groom approached us, and I could see the disappointment in their faces. "We're so sorry," they said. We had no idea the toasts would go so long! Can you guys still play?" "We're happy to play," I said apologetically, "but we've been told we can't go past 10 pm."

We played the first dance, and got in two more dance songs before the venue manager came over to the stage and told us we had to shut it down. The bride and groom pleaded with the manager that we had just started and they had paid all this money for the band and the venue, and it was their *wedding* after all. The manager refused, citing a city ordinance about amplified music not going past a certain hour. "What if we played acoustically?" I interrupted. "That would be fine," she said, "but no amplification." The bride and groom looked at me, puzzled. "Can you do that?" they asked.

"Well, we won't have the keyboard, and the singer will need to sing without a mic. And the bass player and guitar player won't be able to play through their amps. So it'll need to be whisper quiet if you want to hear anything, but we can give it a try," I said.

We unplugged the PA and the amps. The keyboard player picked up a tambourine and played it with her fingers. The bassist and guitarist played their electric instruments with no amplification, and the singer sang without a mic. And I played with my fingers, and an ultra-soft bass drum pedal stroke. I took off my wedding ring and used it to get a sharper, more percussive definition on the hi-hat that was still quiet. We played for an hour and a half, and everybody danced. They gave us a bonus at the end of the night and thanked us profusely for our willingness to play under the circumstances. It was one of the most fun wedding gigs I've ever played.

THE HIGHEST COMPLIMENT

On many occasions after a show, people will come up to me and compliment me on my *playing*. I am always very gracious, and ask if they are drummers too. I try not to take things too much to heart or let my head get any bigger than it should be, but it's certainly always nice to be appreciated. Sometimes people come up to me and compliment me on my *chops*. I don't find this particularly flattering. Just about anybody who practices regularly can gain chops and do impressive things around the drum kit. I'd much rather be appreciated for my musicality. There is one compliment that I do take to heart, and I think it is the highest compliment anyone can give or receive. I hear it only once in a while, which I think makes it all the more meaningful: when someone tells me that my playing was *inspiring*.

Most of the music we make goes out into the world without much evidence of it having an impact in any way. Often, it's just entertainment, consumed in one moment and forgotten the next.

Of course, you never really know what impact your music may have that you don't know about. For the most part, we toil in this business and work so hard because we believe that somehow, what we're doing matters. When a person tells me that he or she was *inspired* by my playing (literally, to exert an animating, enlivening, or exalting influence on; from the Latin *inspirare*, "to breathe into"), it fills me with a deep gratitude and humility to know that my playing had a real impact on someone and might have some small influence on helping them along their path.

THE FUNDAMENTAL IMPORTANCE OF LISTENING

As a musician, your biggest asset is your ability to listen. If you don't listen as you play, you have no idea whether you're in time, in tune, playing too loud or too soft, too busy or too sparsely. Beyond the mechanics of playing with other people, listening and paying close attention helps you have a deeper experience of the music you're playing. It helps you make better music.

Listening is not easy. For many people, it's a skill that needs to be learned. You have to practice focusing your attention in order to be able to direct it to a particular place. Naturally, it takes concentration and attentiveness. It is difficult, if not impossible, to hold that focus all the time. Think of listening as similar to meditation, where the goal is not unwavering concentration the entire time, but an awareness of the moment; the ability to notice what enters the consciousness and let it go by, even if those thoughts are distracting and not apparently pertinent to the experience.

Certainly, over the course of a show, your attention will wander, whether you are performing or sitting in the audience. When you're playing, you need to stay alert and pay attention. I once attended a jazz performance billed as a "Generations" show, with the legendary saxophonist Benny Carter, bass titan Charlie Haden, and a young phenom on piano who will remain nameless; each musician was a formidable talent, from a different generation of players. There was no drummer. (I'd heard Charlie was experiencing some hearing loss, and by that time was hardly playing with drummers anymore.) Charlie has always been an incredibly sensitive player, while the young pianist played with a more muscular approach. Benny was oozing soul the entire night. When it came Charlie's turn to solo, the piano player would stab at chords, comping as a pianist usually would behind the bass solo. Each time, Charlie would hold up his hand, indicating for the pianist to stop playing, which he did. It was clear Charlie was not appreciating the pianist's contributions supporting his solos, and he preferred to play without accompaniment. I don't think it was just a matter of preference. I think it was because the piano player wasn't listening attentively. Charlie's solos were both extremely delicate and harmonically adventurous. The piano player was stepping all over him, hemming him in with chords and voicings that suggested he wasn't following Charlie's ideas. After enough times being humbled on stage, the piano player stopped playing entirely during the bass solos. My guess is the band was assembled as a marketing ploy to bring in a variety of fans of different ages (hence the "Generations" bill), and that they hadn't rehearsed much, if at all.

Nobody likes to play with a selfish player. Nobody wants his or her toes to be stepped on. Musicians, like everybody else, want to be heard, and they want to play with musicians who listen well and are on the same page with what sounds good as a whole.

ON GENIUS AND INNOVATION

People often confuse virtuosity with genius. They're not the same thing. Occasionally they are embodied in the same artist, but often they are not. Many people think saxophonist Charlie Parker was a genius because he played fast runs and a lot of notes in each measure. He was a virtuoso. But Charlie Parker was a genius because he reinvented an approach to jazz improvisation, playing harmonies and phrases that no one had ever played before. It was as if he were playing in three dimensions in what until that time had been a two-dimensional musical landscape. Thelonious Monk was similarly innovative, as were Miles Davis, guitarist Bill Frisell, the Beatles, Led Zeppelin, Radiohead, and many other artists.

Today, every hard-practicing high school sax player can play solos out of the *Charlie Parker Omnibook* and learn his phrasing and rhythmic and harmonic concepts. And while we can debate whether they are able to play with his *soulfulness* and *tone* (they can't), the most important thing is really that Charlie Parker (and Monk, the Beatles, and others) *invented* it. It takes great vision—and perhaps even more courage—to stake out new musical territory. Most of the time, innovative and groundbreaking artists aren't appreciated for their forward-thinking concepts until a number of years later, when, with the benefit of hindsight, we can see how significant and influential their artistry really was.

There are many great bands that have done (primarily) one thing and done it incredibly well. U2 comes to mind, or Green Day, or the Red Hot Chili Peppers. Somehow these groups are able to keep recycling the same thing and make it just a little bit new again—always eminently listenable. Other artists, like Bob Dylan, Miles Davis, Prince, Wayne Shorter, Herbie Hancock, Paul Simon, David Bowie, Led Zeppelin, and the Beatles—evolved much more dramatically, and stayed true to their evolving visions, even in the face of a public—and sometimes a record label—which often wanted them to keep making the same album over and over.

Just because you evolve doesn't make you a genius. But if you follow the creative arc of some of these artists, you can hear their incessant drive for something new, a restless intellectual musical curiosity that ended up pushing them to new heights of creativity that was relevant and influential. It doesn't mean that every one of their efforts was a musical success. But more often than not, they were, and that's why we still listen to them.

FEAR AND COURAGE

Fear is one of the most powerful motivators. It finds its way into so many aspects of our lives, so many of our endeavors, and underpins so many of our interactions with other people. It is insidiously woven into the fabric of our culture through the evening news and through political propaganda. Fear of the unknown can serve an important function, and in some circumstances even save our lives. But more often than not, it holds us back from being the best versions of ourselves that we can be.

In our culture, showing fear or vulnerability is usually considered a sign of weakness. We're taught from a young age to be tough, to "man up"; that it is undesirable to show signs of emotion and vulnerability. Displays of strength and bravado are lionized in movies and television, where our popular cultural heroes appear strong, resilient, unemotional, and unafraid. They endure pain stoically and face every challenge with unwavering determination and courage, and are portrayed as successful precisely because of these traits. This archetype is a caricature. It's not real.

Courage is not the ability to face challenges without fear; it is the determination to face challenges *in spite of being afraid*. Furthermore, trying to live up to such impossible standards is detrimental to our emotional well-being. It handicaps us from honestly assessing our insecurities and processing our emotions, often causing us to bottle up our true feelings until they manifest in less helpful ways—anger, resentment, and suffering.

In reality, many of us respond to displays of vulnerability with compassion and empathy. We even find acts of vulnerability courageous, because we recognize that same vulnerability in ourselves. On some level, just about all of us are afraid that we aren't good enough, that we are not deserving, that we will not be liked, or that we will be judged as somehow inadequate. We seek the approval of our parents and our peers—and for artists, of the greater public.

Every single successful artist I've ever met has at some point in his or her career wrestled with profound self-doubt. Like every other human being, artists want to feel validated for what they do, for the risks they take in creating. Any time you play music with other people or perform in front of an audience, you expose yourself to potential failure and criticism. With improvised music, there is an even greater risk—you never know if you will play inspired, if it will jell. It's a leap of faith every time you play. Performing in front of an audience just ups the ante, especially when expectations are high.

Every path to success is littered with failures. Most good work is not created on the first try. I know many musicians who can't stand to listen back to their early work, who cringe when they hear how immature they sounded as younger players. But the risk-taking, and especially the failures, are the mechanism for our growth. They are absolutely necessary. Without vulnerability, we venture nothing and cannot move forward.

In the 1990s, I attended a clinic at the Music Department at U.C. Berkeley given by the avant-garde jazz saxophonist Steve Coleman. After talking for an hour about how he broke down his approach to playing and composing, he offered the students in attendance a chance to come up and play with his quartet. They played a blues, the universal song form for jazz musicians. It wasn't intended to be a jam session. After one young sax player took a couple of choruses, Steve stopped the band short. "I bet you've played those licks a thousand times," he interrupted. "Play me something that's *right now*, something you've never played before. Not the same old tired licks that you recycle in every jazz solo." Flustered, the horn player nodded his head in embarrassment. As the band resumed and the saxophonist took up his solo again, he fumbled for a bit at first, then began to explore some more interesting ideas. It definitely felt like a work in progress; it also was clear that it was progress toward something more relevant, toward playing more in the moment. It was just an exercise, but it made an impression on me.

The most successful musicians are those who are the most authentic and true to themselves. Look no further than Bob Dylan, one of the greatest poets and songwriters of our time, with what most people would agree is one of the least mellifluous voices to listen to. His earnestness and authenticity are immediately evident in so many of his songs. His artistic voice is unmistakably his. Same with Bruce Springsteen, Paul Simon, James Taylor, Joni Mitchell, Jack White, Kurt Cobain, Johnny Cash, Neil Young, Hank Williams, Antonio Carlos Jobim, Bonnie Raitt, and so many more.

We should be inspired by musicians like these not because we want to be them, but because we should want, like them, to be more like ourselves—transcending self-imposed, fear-based limitations by creating our art. If you feed the monster of self-doubt, it will only grow stronger. If you acknowledge it and don't try to deny it, but instead notice it and choose to focus on your strengths rather than your weaknesses, it can no longer control you and it will not restrain you.

> "Whether 'tis nobler in the mind to suffer
> the slings and arrows of outrageous fortune,
> or to take arms against a sea of troubles,
> and by opposing, end them."
>
> —*William Shakespeare*

THE PATH OF LEAST RESISTANCE

We tend to think of the path of least resistance as a good thing. And why shouldn't we? Who wants to confront conflict or difficulty on the road toward achieving a goal? Shouldn't we strive toward effortlessness and ease? Certainly, the answer is often yes. But sometimes, as we grow accustomed to doing or thinking about things a certain way, the path of least resistance really just becomes *the way that is most comfortable.* And often what is most comfortable is not necessarily in our own best interest. This is especially true when it comes to self-criticism.

We are our own worst critics. We berate ourselves for the mistakes we make, which are often inconsequential. We get so used to looking for all the ways in which we perform inadequately that, to our detriment, we become inured to the process of self-deprecation, which subsequently becomes habituated. We spend so much time fretting about our shortcomings that we miss the big picture and fail to appreciate the magic that we create during live performances.

What's more, many musicians suffer from such insidious insecurity that they reflexively compare their playing to anyone else's they hear. Listening to music thus becomes a competitive sport, with potentially lasting consequences. If every time you go to a show, you're sitting there sizing yourself up against someone else, you're not being a responsible listener. And you're not giving the music the attention that you would like listeners to give it when you perform.

Some musicians even experience this *while* they are playing. Many musicians will get very nervous before they perform. The more experienced ones will usually let go of their fears once they step on stage. But some will continue to let their anxiety get the best of them and distract them from listening. They spend most of their performance worrying about the mistakes they've made (or will make), about what the other musicians are thinking about them, or what the audience is thinking. Or they may fret about that other musician in the audience whom they know is more experienced, or about a teacher or friend they want to impress. No matter what their focus, if it's not on the music and the moment, then they are doing themselves, their fellow musicians, and the audience, a disservice.

I remind my students that their job on stage is to focus on the music. If they let their insecurities get the best of them while they're performing, all they're going to do is ensure that they aren't present. Also, no late cramming is going to help. They're better off trusting the work they've put in to get there, and to let it ride.

I see this also with young kids playing baseball. In Little League, we try to save the skills coaching for practice. At game time, it's all about having fun and playing with the skills you've brought from honing them in practice. When it comes time to perform, the last thing a kid needs is to hear advice about his technique. All this does is put him in his own head and take his focus away from being present in the moment. I've seen it dozens of times—a boy steps up to the plate, nervous and tentative to face the pitcher. Just as he takes his batting stance, a chorus of well-wishing and ignorant parents in the stands gives him about six pieces of advice, one after the other: "Keep your head back." "Level swing!" "Elbow up!" "Watch your timing!" "Don't drop your shoulder!"...all of which are worse than useless. Not only do they often conflict with one another (or with what we coaches have spent many hours trying to teach them), they also cause the child to doubt himself, and to stay in his critical mind instead of being in the moment.

Kids feel enormous pressure to perform well, especially when their parents are watching. Hitting a baseball is as difficult for kids as it is for professional hitters. Trying to incorporate more than one piece of (usually bad) advice is a recipe for disaster. Inevitably these kids strike out, which only leads to more parental advice shouted louder from the stands. It can get so bad that sometimes even when the parents are keeping quiet, the kids have learned to play that soundtrack in their heads. It can take a whole season to teach a kid to trust his skills and to just try to have fun and be in the moment when they play. Many professional ballplayers still work on this very thing.

And so it often is with music. The path of least resistance is often the mental path that has become the most grooved through repetition. And often it doesn't turn out to be the path of low resistance at all, but a self-limiting approach that predisposes musicians to put up a mental barrier and play from their critical minds, instead of from the heart.

* * *

One summer night during the 1990s, I had a gig with my jazz quartet at a hotel bar in Berkeley. There were a handful of folks nursing drinks at their tables and a few more at the bar, but there was one couple who got up in front of the band and wanted to dance. "Do you play swing music?" the woman asked.

At the time, there had been a resurgence in popularity of the jump-swing music of the 1940s, and the venue was booking swing dance music several nights a week. I assumed this couple came because they were expecting to hear Glenn Miller.

"We're a little more diverse," I replied, "a little more modern." I was nervous already. The thing was, our music wasn't really danceable. It was more "listening jazz," swinging at times, but more explorative with a wider range of feels. Definitely not jump swing.

"But can you play swing?" the man asked. "We want to dance!" the woman exclaimed.

Before we'd even played a note, I felt like we were a wedding band trying to satisfy an obnoxious aunt and uncle who keep requesting their favorite song. We started with a swinging version of Miles Davis' "Solar." I knew it wasn't what they were looking for. After each tune we played, they would implore again us to play some jump swing. My insecurity grew with each passing song. *We're the wrong band for this venue. Maybe we should play some straight-ahead stuff so they can dance. I shouldn't have booked this gig. Man, this gig sucks.*

It wasn't until the break that I realized that my head was spinning with doubt. I'd even called "C Jam Blues" in an effort to give the couple what they wanted. (To my relief, they did dance to that one.) When I stepped outside for some air, I caught myself. *What was I doing?* The talent buyer had booked my quartet based on the CD I'd sent them. The venue knew what they were getting. They wanted what we had to offer. *Why should we try to be something different, other than what we were?* It was just one persistent couple that set off this whole avalanche of self-doubt. Worst of all, I was not enjoying playing. I was in my head the entire time, and I wasn't paying attention to the music.

And then it hit me: if I kept on like that, the only feeling I was going to walk away with was that I had a miserable gig. *Wrong band, wrong venue, they didn't like us.* I had a choice. It was within my power to change my attitude and change my experience. So I did.

I went back in after the break, and we played our original music. I decided I didn't care about the couple that so desperately wanted to dance, and who soon left. Rid of the distractions from the first set, I played the rest of the night entirely focused on the music. The band felt it too. We ended up having a great night, and the remaining audience, scant as it was, was very enthusiastic. I had turned a bad gig into a good one just by catching myself going down the path of least resistance and making a decision to change my experience.

VISION AND LEADERSHIP

I lead a number of bands. I am the Co-Director and Co-Founder of a successful multi-city rock and roll after-school and summer camp program. I've run a music camp, worked as an artistic director and a program coordinator, and hired and fired staff. I've started several different small businesses, created a music teachers' cooperative, and been on the board of a non-profit arts organization. In all of these different experiences, I've found that there are two distinct types of leadership: leadership based on approval, and leadership based on vision.

Whether it's a band or a business, I believe all organizations need to have a leader with a vision and the skills and internal resources to execute that vision. This alone doesn't guarantee success, but it's very difficult to succeed without it. You also need to know how to delegate and surround yourself with a team that supports your vision and can help you bring it to fruition.

When I was younger and less confident, one of my main concerns in leading a band was that the players I played with liked me. I was always deferential to what other people wanted, and though I would offer my opinions, I didn't lead my band based on any focused idea of what I wanted it to sound like. Nor did I have any kind of realistic goals, other than vague notions of commercial success as defined by things like record deals, tours, and endorsements. Even with those loosely-framed ideals floating around in my mind, I had no real understanding of the steps needed to attain them. They weren't really goals, more like the idea of what I thought goals should look or sound like, if that makes sense.

Similarly, when I first took over the job of running a music camp in my late twenties, I was very concerned with obtaining approval from the community, though I didn't realize it at the time. I wanted to be seen as someone who was capable and responsible, and I wanted to make people happy. As any business leader can tell you, it's nearly impossible to please everybody. People have different needs, and in satisfying one person you often leave another's needs unmet. Every strategic and programming decision has a potential chain reaction of repercussions, and if your primary goal is to make people happy by catering to their whims, you are going to end up scrambling to fix a cascade of problems that will end up leading to a dysfunctional organization. It took me three years to truly realize that and shift my focus toward creating a vision to help the camp grow and serve the community better.

The most effective leaders act based on their informed and carefully cultivated vision for success and commitment to healthy evolution. Even if your business has no aspirations to grow beyond a mom and pop operation, you will always need to evolve and stay current with changes in commerce and culture.

As in business, so it is with music. So many of my young students want to play in bands. Most of them don't even know how to find other kids to play with. A few manage to arrange a time to get together with friends to play (no small feat these days, with sports, martial arts, lessons, tutors, and other commitments taking up their scant unstructured time). They gather at the drummer's house, only to discover that they don't know what to play. There's a lot of "I don't know, what do you want to play...I don't know, what do *you* want to play?" They may end up scratching around the edges of a handful of tunes or jamming on some simple chord progressions. Sometimes that's just great, and it can be the first steps toward something more. Often that ends up being the last step, because kids, for the most part, don't yet have any crystallized musical ideas. They don't know what they want to play, let alone what they want to do with a band, other than knowing that they want to be *in* a band. Many of my younger students have told me they were in a band—they even had a band name, and had already worked out a band t-shirt design. When I ask them what kind of music they play, they admit that they don't know, as the band hasn't actually played together yet.

I've seen this situation play out with adult bands too, though it usually looks a little different. Bands get together and hash out their favorite rock covers; after a few months, they start to get bored with the same-old-same-old. Often, these bands will stall out without a musician who has a clearer vision for what they want to play, a sound they want to create, an identity they want to form.

When I first moved to the Bay Area in the early '90s, I wanted to get in on the jazz scene. I played at a few jam sessions and waited for my phone to ring, which it did on occasion. I didn't have any idea of what I really wanted to play, other than that I wanted to play out. I played some gigs with a number of different players, but never really felt like I found my niche. In retrospect, I believe that was because I didn't really have a clear idea for what I wanted to do. It wasn't until I had the chance to really evolve musically and experiment with different groups on my own gigs that I felt like I began to form a coherent concept of what I was after. And from that vision, I started on the path to create a band and record several albums.

Sometimes a creative concept can be born from a fortuitous alignment of people in the right place at the right time; the idea for a band can come out of a conversation, or a jam session, or a gig that brought people together who had great chemistry. Similarly, you can come across other individuals who have a creative vision in mind and you can align your focus together. After all, in a band, not everybody can be the bandleader or creative force behind the music. Usually the drummer is not the songwriter or composer (with some notable exceptions), and will play a support role (no less important!) in helping the band reach its creative potential. A successful project involves each individual contributing his or her strengths, balanced to achieve harmony.

It's easy to know you want to play in a band, or headline a show, or record an album, or be on the cover of a magazine. It's a lot more difficult to conceive of an artistic vision for creating something that comes from the heart. That usually comes from life experience, soul searching, experimentation, and nurturing the artistic spark that lies within each of us—and a lot of hard work. If it were easy, everyone would do it.

HOW WE LISTEN TO MUSIC AND WHY IT MATTERS

I read a very insightful book called *How Music Works* by David Byrne, the lead singer and creative force behind the band The Talking Heads. In it, Byrne suggests that what we often assert to be a composer's "genius" is more often a confluence of the right things happening at the right time, in the right venue or medium, and for the right audience. I think he's spot-on. He also asserts that the context in which we listen to music—literally, the actual venue or locale—has a tremendous impact on not just how music is consumed, but how music is created.

To summarize his point: when early music was heard in cathedrals, with tall marble ceilings and airy listening spaces with a lot of echo and reverb, the music had to sound pleasing to the ear in such a unique space. Modal chants worked well because they didn't sound unpleasant when one note would sustain in the virtual echo chamber of the church and another would be sung on top of it. All the notes reverberating together didn't clash with one another. As music moved into smaller venues, and parlors and listening rooms became the most common venues for hearing live music, composers were able to explore more sophisticated harmonic constructs and complex contrapuntal approaches, since they no longer needed to worry about notes sustaining uncontrollably and conflicting with one another. It kept evolving from there, with listening venues and modalities affecting how composers and bands wrote and performed live music throughout the past several centuries.

In the 1970s and early '80s, everybody was listening to music on cassettes or vinyl. (My parents still had an 8-track player at the time, but the only thing I listened to as a kid on the 8-track was the *Star Wars* soundtrack.) Mostly, you'd play your cassettes on your portable boom box. The second generation of those boom boxes had bass boost buttons, because the bass was practically inaudible on those cheap, small, low-fi speakers. (The bass boost buttons didn't really make the low end any clearer, just louder.) Most of the popular music of the 1970s was fairly bright sounding, with a lot of hi-hats and guitars. It was punchy, and it cut through the cheap stereo speakers, boom boxes, and portable cassette players that were the primary listening devices of the day. I'm not suggesting that the advent of the portable cassette player was necessarily the driving force behind how these albums were mixed, but there is no doubt that the medium through which people listen to music has at least some impact on how it is recorded, and mixed, in the studio.

Consider that most modern recording studios have several different sets of reference monitors through which to listen to mixes. These speakers act to offer a range of possible different listening environments, from the small bookshelf speakers popular in the '90s to the larger speakers that produce more bass frequencies. In any case, any producer or engineer will tell a recording artist when listening to their mixes, to go and listen on their car stereo and whatever device they normally listen to music on—computer, smartphone, home system, or headphones. Because these are the media through which people listen nowadays, you need to mix the music to sound good on those media. It doesn't really mean much if a recording is perfectly balanced on a pair of $10,000 speakers, when nobody will be listening to the music on those speakers. So, when we're considering mixes, we listen the way most people listen, and make adjustments to suit how it sounds on our devices.

* * *

When CDs first came out, they sounded much brighter and punchier than records. (The first CD I ever bought was Boston's *Boston*, I'm proud to say.) All of a sudden you could hear so much more detail. As an adult, I can totally get behind the argument that there was a warmth on vinyl that was lost on CDs. But you really do need a high-quality turntable to hear both the clarity and the warmth, whereas CDs brought that clarity to the masses even if at the expense of some of the intimacy of vinyl.

In my twenties, I became interested in listening to music on high-fidelity systems. I'd go with my friend to these boutique stereo shops where they'd only have one pair of speakers in each room, because we were told having a second pair, even unplugged, would adversely affect the sound. We'd sit and listen to our favorite CDs and albums, trying to discern every nuance we could. We'd debate the low-end punchy-ness of various speakers and argue about which turntable sounded the warmest. I never had the money to afford a high-end system, so I settled for more reasonably-priced consumer components. For better or worse, the medium I ended up with, a mid-range home stereo system, served me for a number of formative years as I listened to music voraciously and educated myself throughout my twenties and thirties.

About once a month, I'd trek out over to Amoeba Records on Telegraph Avenue in Berkeley and buy about $150 worth of mostly used vinyl and CDs. I filled glaring holes in my musical exposure (Stevie Wonder, Howlin' Wolf, the Meters, Tom Waits, Desmond Dekker, Nina Simone, Albert Collins, Sonny Stitt), and dug deeper into lesser known artists (Abdullah Ibrahim, Los Van Van, Snooks Eaglin, Baaba Maal, David Lindley, Clifton Chenier), in addition to digging what was new and happening (White Stripes, Me'Shell Ndegeocello, the Roots, the Shins, Charlie Hunter). It was a fertile time for me, mainly because I had the time to devote to listening before the real responsibilities of adulthood set in. I listened on my stereo system, which was my primary window to the world of music.

I still listen to music of course, but I don't consume new music as voraciously as I once did. I also no longer have my stereo system. Instead I check new things out mostly on the Internet, on streaming listening services or on YouTube or iTunes. On rare occasions, I'll buy a new CD, but it's usually to support an artist at a live show. There's still something satisfying about holding the medium in your hands, as opposed to everything being digital—plus you get the added bonus of the album artwork, liner notes, and a list of the musicians on each track.

I believe in the superior audio quality of vinyl and CDs over the compressed mp3 file, despite my (mostly) having gone along with the inevitable changes to the industry and the modern models for music consumption. I believe it's unfortunate that musicians and record companies (should they really be called record companies anymore?) spend so much time and money making music in the studio sound so good, only to have so much of the original detail lost in compression so we can carry 10,000 songs with us everywhere we go, or stream vast catalogs of music with the click of a button. In exchange for portability and ease of access, we have sacrificed quality, richness, and nuance (to say nothing of equitable compensation for the artists). And maybe, just maybe, that's had an influence on the "correctness" of much of modern popular music, which has been scoured of the mistakes, elasticity, and shading that captured the wider, more soulful range of human expression. Instead we have pitch-perfect, auto-tuned vocalists and drum machines, and over-produced, artificially clean pop music, which is perfect for listening to in a digitally compressed format. Thankfully, there is still a dedicated subset of artists who have resisted this trend.

MISTAKES…AND WHAT WE'RE AFTER
WHEN WE'RE PLAYING

The better you get, the fewer "mistakes" you make. In my early twenties, I would actually count the number of mistakes I made during a show. It was usually four or five. They'd typically be little things, like a bass drum figure I didn't quite nail, or a fill that was a little rushed. My goal was to be perfect, to get my mistakes total down to zero. I don't know if I ever got it down to zero, but I do know that I stopped caring, and I stopped thinking about music as a zero-mistake sum game.

At the top levels of popular live music, musicians' parts are all very carefully crafted and expertly executed. But that doesn't mean that there are no mistakes. It just means you didn't notice them. The better you get, the subtler your "mistakes" become, to the point where usually you (and possibly your bandmates) are the only ones noticing them. Most mistakes are moments. And while a show is made up of so many moments, one moment never defines a show, or even a song, unless there's a wardrobe malfunction.

In many early rock and R&B recordings, you can hear all sorts of mistakes. Because most early recordings were made live in the studio, bands and producers didn't have the modern luxury of being able to punch in and fix individual notes or smooth out passages. The music was recorded all at once, and sometimes included clearly recognizable, inadvertent musical errors. There were warts all over the place. If the song was otherwise a good performance on tape, it didn't matter.

In jazz, mistakes can often be a source of inspiration. I've heard many jazz players hit a "wrong" note, only to decide to hit it again and turn it into a creative statement. Miles Davis was well known for this. The great tenor sax player Coleman Hawkins once said, "If you're not making mistakes, you're not trying hard enough." What a beautiful, liberating way of thinking about playing music. Especially in jazz, where the music is largely improvised, mistakes are a part of the territory. In fact, I'd even say that calling them "mistakes" is a misnomer. They're just moments. They may be moments when you didn't execute exactly what you intended, but that doesn't necessarily make it a bad moment. "Mistake" implies a value judgment that doesn't always need to be there. Just because something was unintended doesn't necessarily make it wrong.

I have some students who are so petrified of making errors that they will only play the absolute simplest thing, for fear of being wrong. Even when I encourage them to think of the practice studio as a safe place for making mistakes and explain that mistakes help them get better, they still have a hard time letting go. Once we pass a certain age, it's hard-wired in our brains. Kids don't seem to have the same hang up. They'll play loud and make all kinds of mistakes, because they have no fear, no expectation of what they are supposed to sound like. Adults, on the other hand, are often burdened by some past experience when making a mistake caused them some emotional pain or embarrassment. It's not an easy thing to get over.

I used to cringe when I made mistakes. Now I smile. I catch the bass player's eye and make a funny face, and we laugh. Or maybe I catch her making one and it's the same thing. We don't care about them (unless of course there's some arrangement issue that represents a misunderstanding that needs to be cleared up in rehearsal). And if by some small chance someone in the audience noticed it, we've showed them how they should feel about it. Don't make a sour face in distaste, or you're telegraphing to the audience that they should wince too.

So if it's not perfect, mistake-free renditions of our songs we're truly after when we play, what are we after? *Connecting with an audience.* And how do we do that? By playing with energy and authenticity. Whenever one of my students comes in and tells me about a great show they saw, I always ask him, "What made it so good? Why did you enjoy it so much?" The answer is almost always the same; something along the lines of, "The band played with such great energy. They blew me away. They really seemed to have so much fun on stage." We respond to the energy and authenticity of a musical performance more than anything.

Remember that music, in addition to being artistic expression, is also entertainment. People go to shows because they want to connect to the music and to the musicians and to share the experience of hearing the music with other people. As a musician, it's your job to create that connection by bringing your best and playing with enthusiasm and sincerity. Nobody wants to watch a band phone it in. I've been to several shows like that, where the musicians didn't really seem to be enjoying playing. They'd look off into the distance, sport a grumpy countenance, and really just give the impression that they'd rather be somewhere else.

Contrast that with a performer like Bruce Springsteen. If you've ever been to a Boss show, you know he is one of the best performers of the modern era. He puts on a great show every time, always plays a marathon set, and he pours out his soul into every performance. And so does his band. They're playing the same songs night after night, but to an audience that is there for the first and only time. The audience wants the best he has to offer, and he delivers like it's the first night every time, a peak performance. What an incredible professional.

Don't get caught up in your mistakes. Remember what you're after is a good and memorable show, with a transcendent connection with the audience, no matter how big or small. Bring everything you've got, and pour it into your music just like Bruce does, whether it's in a living room or on an arena stage. If you do, nobody will remember the mistakes.

EFFORTLESS MASTERY

In 1996, jazz pianist Kenny Werner wrote a book called *Effortless Mastery*, a treatise on the mental approach to playing music. I attended a couple of his clinics in my early thirties when he was out in the Bay Area. His wisdom and approach have stayed with me since then and have had a very constructive and positive influence on my attitude toward playing music. They've also influenced the way I teach.

In his book, Kenny describes the ego-based thinking and insecurities that get in the way of playing the best music we're capable of. He suggests that the self-conscious editing brain, once engaged, ends up limiting our potential for the most fluid, deeply connected, inspired, and effortless playing. This removes us from the ideal mental space for artistic expression: that of unconscious, "unself-aware" channeling of the artistry that is inside all of us. We get caught up in wanting to play well or *thinking* about playing well—or about not playing well—and in that attachment to the *result* of our playing, we remove ourselves from the "space," or the "zone," of unconscious reflexive *doing*, which allows us to play most freely and relaxed. Once our analytical brain gets involved with expectation, attachment to results, or analysis of our playing in real time, it disrupts our natural ability to just "do" in the most pure and unadulterated way.

This phenomenon is not unique to music, and it is an intrinsic tenet of the practice of Zen. (In fact, Kenny's book includes a number of meditation exercises to help train yourself to get into the "space." I can appreciate the idea and believe it can be transformative for some people.) I've experienced this same thing in the context of sports. In golf, if you start thinking too much about your swing *while you're swinging*, you can pretty much ensure that you won't strike the ball well. Likewise in baseball and archery. We practice and practice, and we hone our body/brain connection through countless repetitions to be able to execute a very specialized task at a high level of proficiency, whether it's improvising intelligible music, hitting a golf ball squarely, or nailing a jump shot. Even after all that practice, we often let our minds get in the way of what our bodies know how to do—particularly when we're under pressure and need to perform at a high level. It's very difficult to let go, especially when we have such a strong desire to perform well. In my decades of performing in public, I can say with surety that I play my best when I am most relaxed.

* * *

I vividly remember playing golf one early morning when the fog still clung thick to the hillsides at Tilden Park in the Berkeley hills.

You could barely see more than 40 or 50 yards ahead, so just about every shot was blind, into the white abyss. I had played the course many times, so knew generally where to aim, but I had such low expectations of playing well under the conditions (in fact, I figured I'd be unable to find my ball half the time, not being able to see where it went), that I just decided to enjoy the morning walk through the fog and swing free and easy.

For about 12 holes, I was playing the best golf of my life. I think I was just under par. Every shot sailed just as I intended it to, and my putting was equally relaxed and efficient. I was striking the ball perfectly every swing. The longer the round went, the more I started to become aware that I was playing as well as I had ever played. I started thinking about the score I might achieve, which would surely be a personal best. And right around that time, about two-thirds of the way through the round, the sun came out. Finally, I could see where my shots were going and could take more precise aim at my targets.

It happened slowly at first—an errant tee shot, a missed putt, a bogey, then a double. Then a meltdown hole. Up until the sun came out, I had been playing as relaxed as I'd ever played, unattached to the results of my golf shots because I had no expectations or strong desire to play well; *I was just enjoying playing*. As I began to think about my score and started caring about where my shots flew, I started playing worse. I began to make mental calculations about what score I needed on each hole to reach a certain goal at the end of the round. I started thinking about *not* making mistakes, which is the same as thinking about making mistakes. And I made them. I ended up with a good score, but it wasn't a personal best, and it was a huge disappointment from the expectations and hopes I had created for myself part way through the round.

Often, the harder we try to do well at something, the worse we do. I do my best to convey this concept to my students in reference to performing, and even to how they "perform" at their lessons. (Despite my efforts to make the lesson studio feel like a safe and supportive environment, some students can't help but feel like they have to perform for their teacher.) I remind them to focus on the enjoyment of playing music when they're on stage, in the same way that they enjoy it without thinking when they're not in front of people; that the more they listen to the music and stay focused in the moment, the more they will enjoy the experience of making music and the more likely that they will end up feeling good about their playing.

"WHAT IS SUCCESS?"
–Allen Toussaint

It's easy to want to be successful. We all have hopes and dreams, and most musicians at some point fantasize about hitting the big time, playing the marquee shows, scoring the lucrative record deal. Just like every Little Leaguer dreams of pitching in the World Series one day, even if 99.9% of them know they'll never get there. Many musicians have gone through some kind of phase like this, especially when they were younger. Big dreams have to start somewhere, and some people will rise to the top of their chosen pursuit through talent, luck, resourcefulness, and mostly, hard work.

As you mature and begin to examine your life more thoughtfully, it becomes more challenging to define for yourself what success really means. I know many musicians who, by every reasonable metric, would be considered successful. They have toured, secured endorsements and record deals, played with famous bands, and made a living from their music. But some of them are miserable. They come home exhausted from touring, missing their spouses and kids or longing for a stable relationship, and often not much better off financially than when they left. Some are fed up with dysfunctional band members or dishonest managers, exploitative promoters and label executives.

Many musicians who dream of making the big time really haven't thought through what "making it" really means. If money isn't the motivation, then what is? Fame? While most famous musicians may enjoy their success, for some, it's not all fun. When you are instantly recognizable, it can be difficult to walk down the street without being constantly accosted by people or hounded by paparazzi. It's no wonder so many celebrities retreat into a cocoon of inaccessibility and keep everybody but their closest friends at arm's length. Everything has a trade off, and most musicians don't consider this when they dream of being successful.

I went through some soul-searching around this as a young adult. I'd harbored these notions of success without really defining for myself what it really meant. Turns out for me, I'm after playing music that I like playing and that people like listening to. I want to open people's minds and inspire them. Gigs are often exhilarating, touring can be fun and rewarding, and some notoriety can be great for your ego, not to mention your wallet. But those are just the party favors that come with the real prize—changing people's lives through music.

When my students and friends pose these existential questions about pursuing musical (or other kinds of) success, I tell them that a good rule of thumb is to continue to ask yourself the question "why" after you think you've answered what success means for you. For example, you might think, "*If only I could get an endorsement, I would be successful.*" Why? What would obtaining an endorsement mean for you? That you get free drums? That's mostly a pipe dream, even with an endorsement. Landing a record deal is an admirable goal. But what does that achievement mean? That people like your music? That you are making a living just playing music? Those things are achievable without a record deal. Would it mean that you are a good drummer? Or would it be a feather in your cap to show off that you've made it to the big time? It might just as easily mean none of those things. The same goes for playing at Madison Square Garden, or making the cover of *Modern Drummer*. These things are great accolades, to be sure. But do they define success? Ultimately, it's up to you to figure that out for yourself.

Be careful what you wish for—because the reality of achieving your success might not end up making you happy if you haven't really thought it through. For many people, if they keep asking "why," the answer comes down to deeper, more meaningful things like playing the best music you are capable of, or connecting with others through music, or playing for people whose lives you want to impact. Or maybe offering some respite or hope of escape from the vicissitudes of life through artistic expression, connecting performer and audience through a fleeting but transcendent bond.

The great jazz drummer Art Blakey said, "Jazz washes away the dust of everyday life." This was actually a reworking of an earlier quote from Berthold Auerbach, the 19th century German-Jewish writer, who said, "Music washes away from the soul the dust of everyday life." And perhaps, in the end, when you strip away all the bullshit and ego, that's what music can be at its best—cleansing, healing…a unique bond that connects us as humans and illuminates our shared experiences, our suffering and our joy.

ACKNOWLEDGMENTS

I would like to thank the many people without whose encouragement and support this book would never have come to fruition. My deepest gratitude to my wife, Michele Friedman, for her unwavering support of my writing, teaching, and performing—and also for typesetting the book and designing the cover. Thank you to my sister, Manya Steinkoler, for her close, insightful reading, and to Wendy Horng Brawer for her thoughtful comments and invaluable help with organization. Thank you to Caroline White and Jeffrey Shapiro for their feedback, and to Jody Lerner for her proofreading. I am grateful to the good people at the Editorial Department, specifically Ross Browne for his support of the book, and Julie Miller for her editing expertise and candor. Special thanks to Charylu Roberts for her advice, and to Ronny Schiff for helping me get to the final draft and for her patience and guidance through the revision process. My sincere appreciation to Rob Wallis and Joe Bergamini at Hudson Music for bringing me on board, and for their enthusiasm about this book.

I wouldn't be where I am as a drummer without the guidance, patience, and support of my teachers: Mark Vereggee, who got me started when I was 10 years old, and Norman Grossman, who inspired me as a teenager with his knowledge and musicality. I'd also like to thank Victor Lewis, George Johnson III, Eddie Marshall, and Paul van Wageningen, who gave me help in small doses as I needed it as a professional. Much love to Jamie Rusling, who got me started teaching before I even knew what I was doing, nor how much I would come to love it. I offer sincere and humble gratitude to my musical peers, who have shaped my playing in more ways than they could know.

I am indebted to Chris Brady at Aquarian Drumheads, Mike Damico at Brooks Drums, Dean Bowdery at Protection Racket, and all the people at Vic Firth Drumsticks for their material support over the years, as well as for their support of this book. Heartfelt thanks to David Garibaldi, Dawn Richardson, and Dom Famularo for their advance readings of the manuscript, and for their encouragement.

I'd also like to thank my past and current students, who have taught me so many valuable lessons over the years. This book is for you.

APPENDIX

MY FAVORITE DRUMMERS
(in no particular order)

*(Primary band[s] or artist[s] they performed and/or
recorded with in parentheses)*

Brian Blade *(Wayne Shorter, Joshua Redman, Joni Mitchell,
Herbie Hancock, et al.)*

Bill Stewart *(Maceo Parker, John Scofield, Pat Metheny)*

Max Roach *(Charlie Parker, Clifford Brown, Miles Davis,
Duke Ellington, Thelonious Monk, et al.)*

Elvin Jones *(John Coltrane, Charles Mingus, Miles Davis, et al.)*

Jack DeJohnette *(Keith Jarrett, Bill Evans, Miles Davis,
Herbie Hancock, John Scofield, et al.)*

"Papa" Jo Jones *(Count Basie, Duke Ellington, et al.)*

"Philly Joe" Jones *(Miles Davis, Bill Evans, Sonny Rollins, et al.)*

Roy Haynes *(Chick Corea, Pat Metheny, Miles Davis, Stan Getz,
Sonny Stitt, Gary Burton, et al.)*

Zakir Hussain *(Mickey Hart, John McLaughlin, Alla Rakha,
Béla Fleck, L. Shankar, et al.)*

John Bonham *(Led Zeppelin)*

Steve Gadd *(Paul Simon, Steely Dan, James Taylor, Joe Cocker,
Chick Corea, Frank Sinatra, Paul McCartney, Eric Clapton,
B.B. King, Kate Bush, et al.)*

Jim Keltner *(George Harrison, John Lennon, Leon Russell, John Hiatt, Ry Cooder, J.J. Cale, Richard Thompson, Neil Young, Booker T. & the M.G.s, Bob Dylan, Simon & Garfunkel, Steve Miller, et al.)*

J.R. Robinson *(Michael Jackson, Eric Clapton, Madonna, Steve Winwood, George Benson, Quincy Jones, John Fogerty, Natalie Cole, Pointer Sisters, et al.)*

Roger Hawkins *(Muscle Shoals Rhythm Section, Aretha Franklin, Percy Sledge, Wilson Pickett, Paul Simon, Bob Seger, The Staple Singers, et al.)*

Benny Benjamin *(The Funk Brothers—Motown Records rhythm section)*

Richard "Pistol" Allen *(The Funk Brothers—Motown Records rhythm section)*

Uriel Jones *(The Funk Brothers—Motown Records rhythm section)*

Hal Blaine *("The Wrecking Crew"—house band for producer Phil Spector, Elvis Presley, the Beach Boys, Simon & Garfunkel, The Byrds, Frank Sinatra, Nancy Sinatra, The Carpenters, The 5th Dimension, Neil Diamond, Johnny Cash, Ray Charles, John Denver, Ike & Tina Turner, et al.)*

Al Jackson, Jr. *(Booker T. & the M.G.'s—Stax Records rhythm section, Otis Redding, Sam & Dave, Albert King, Rufus Thomas, Al Green, Tina Turner, Eric Clapton, Rod Stewart, Donny Hathaway, et al.)*

Kenny Clarke *(Charlie Parker, Dizzy Gillespie, Thelonious Monk, Modern Jazz Quartet, Miles Davis)*

Nigel Olsson *(Elton John)*

Jon Christensen *(Keith Jarrett)*

Greg Errico *(Sly & the Family Stone)*

Sly Dunbar *(Peter Tosh, The Mighty Diamonds, Compass Point All Stars studio band)*

Jim Capaldi *(Traffic, Jimi Hendrix, Eric Clapton, Cat Stevens)*

Manu Katché *(Peter Gabriel, Sting, Jeff Beck, Simple Minds, Tears for Fears, Dire Straits, Tori Amos, et al.)*

Richie Hayward *(Little Feat, Eric Clapton, Ry Cooder, James Cotton, Doobie Brothers, Bob Dylan, Peter Frampton, Buddy Guy, Taj Mahal, et al.)*

Levon Helm *(The Band)*

Pick Withers *(Dire Straits)*

Pete Thomas *(Elvis Costello & the Attractions)*

Al Foster *(Miles Davis, Herbie Hancock, Sonny Rollins, McCoy Tyner, Joe Henderson, et al.)*

Victor Lewis *(Kenny Barron, Carla Bley, Stan Getz, Woody Shaw, et al.)*

Ndugu Chancler *(Eddie Harris, Harold Land, Weather Report, Michael Jackson, George Duke, Carlos Santana, Lionel Richie, George Benson, The Temptations, Herbie Hancock, et al.)*

Stewart Copeland *(The Police)*

Clyde Stubblefield *(James Brown)*

John "Jabo" Starks *(James Brown)*

Melvin Parker *(James Brown, Maceo Parker)*

Mitch Mitchell *(Jimi Hendrix)*

Herlin Riley *(Ahmad Jamal, Wynton Marsalis, George Benson, Harry Connick, Jr., et al.)*

Harvey Mason *(Herbie Hancock's Headhunters, Chick Corea, Bob James, the Brecker Brothers, George Benson, Donna Summer, John Legend, Robben Ford, Bill Withers, et al.)*

Steve Ferrone *(Tom Petty & the Heartbreakers, Average White Band, Chaka Khan, Duran Duran, Eric Clapton, Johnny Cash, Bee Gees, et al.)*

Bernard Purdie *(James Brown, Aretha Franklin, Steely Dan, David "Fathead" Newman, Eddie Harris and Les McCann, Hubert Laws, Herbie Mann, Miles Davis, B.B. King, Hall & Oates, Cat Stevens, Houston Person, et al.)*

Kenny Buttrey *(Bob Dylan, Neil Young, Jimmy Buffett)*

Jerome "Bigfoot" Brailey *(Parliament/Funkadelic)*

Peter Erskine *(Weather Report, Steps Ahead, Stan Kenton, Maynard Ferguson, Bob Mintzer, John Abercrombie, Gary Burton, Jaco Pastorius, Joni Mitchell, Diana Krall, et al.)*

Herman "Roscoe" Ernest, III *(Dr. John, Snooks Eaglin, Etta James, Earl King, Marcia Ball, Neville Brothers, Kermit Ruffins, Allen Toussaint, et al.)*

Martin Chambers *(The Pretenders)*

Carlton Barrett *(Bob Marley & the Wailers)*

Eric Harland *(Charles Lloyd, Dave Holland, Joshua Redman, et al.)*

Steve Smith *(Journey, Vital Information, Mariah Carey, Jean-Luc Ponty, et al.)*

Evelyn Glennie *(Scottish Chamber Orchestra, Björk, Béla Fleck, Bobby McFerrin, Fred Frith, Mark Knopfler)*

Ahmir "?uestlove" Thompson *(The Roots, Tonight Show Band)*

Joseph "Zigaboo" Modeliste *(The Meters)*

David Garibaldi *(Tower of Power)*

Joe Morello *(Dave Brubeck, Gary Burton)*

Trilok Gurtu *(Gary Moore, John McLaughlin, Oregon, Jan Garbarek, Joe Zawinul, et al.)*

Jeff Ballard *(Chick Corea, Brad Mehldau, Pat Metheny, Kurt Rosenwinkel, Avishai Cohen)*

Omar Hakim *(David Bowie, Sting, Madonna, Dire Straits, Kate Bush, Miles Davis, Mariah Carey, Celine Dion, et al.)*

Gregory Hutchinson *(Joshua Redman, Ray Brown, Oscar Peterson, Roy Hargrove, et al.)*

Roger Taylor *(Queen)*

Stanton Moore *(Galactic, Garage a Trois, Robert Walter, et al.)*

Dawn Richardson *(4 Non-Blondes, Tracy Chapman, Shana Morrison, et al.)*

Billy Higgins *(Ornette Coleman, Lee Morgan, Donald Byrd, Joe Henderson, Dexter Gordon, Grant Green, Thelonious Monk, David Murray, Art Farmer, Charlie Haden, Eddie Harris, Jackie McLean, Hank Mobley, Cedar Walton, Art Pepper, et al.)*

Kenny Wollesen *(Bill Frisell, Tom Waits, Norah Jones, Sex Mob)*

Paul Motian *(Bill Evans, Keith Jarrett, Bill Frisell, Joe Lovano, Don Cherry, Charlie Haden, Chick Corea, et al.)*

Earl Palmer *(Little Richard, Fats Domino, Professor Longhair, The Monkees, the Mamas & the Papas, Elvis Costello, The Beach Boys, Sam Cooke, Bobby Day, Shirley and Lee, The Righteous Brothers, Eddie Cochran, Johnny Otis, Ike & TinaTurner, Tom Waits, et al.)*

Johnny Vidacovich *(Astral Project, Bobby McFerrin, Robert Walter, Professor Longhair, James Booker, Mose Allison, et al.)*

Ringo Starr *(The Beatles)*

Jeffrey "Jellybean" Alexander *(Jon Cleary & the Absolute Monster Gentlemen, Papa Grows Funk, Snooks Eaglin, The Wild Magnolias)*

Charlie Watts *(The Rolling Stones)*

Jeff "Tain" Watts *(Wynton Marsalis, Branford Marsalis, McCoy Tyner, Alice Coltrane, Betty Carter, Michael Brecker, et al.)*

Glenn Kotche *(Wilco)*

Justin Brown *(Thundercat, Christian McBride, Esperanza Spalding, Vijay Iyer, et al.)*

Antonio Sanchez *(Pat Metheny)*

Robert "Sput" Searight *(Snarky Puppy)*

John Mader *(Joshua Redman, Bonnie Raitt, Randy Newman, Steve Miller, Booker T., The Family Stone, Hamilton: an American Musical, et al.)*

Grady Tate *(Jimmy Smith, Quincy Jones, Ella Fitzgerald, Stan Getz, Wes Montgomery, Duke Ellington, Count Basie, et al.)*

Michael Urbano *(Smash Mouth, John Hiatt, Cracker, Third Eye Blind, Paul Westerberg, Camper Van Beethoven, Neil Finn, Sheryl Crow, Luciano Ligabue, et al.)*

Ed Thigpen *(Oscar Peterson, Billy Taylor, Ella Fitzgerald, Dexter Gordon, et al.)*

Idris Muhammad *(Ahmad Jamal, Pharoah Sanders, Gene Ammons, Sam Cooke, Fats Domino, Houston Person, George Benson, Lou Donaldson, Grant Green, et al.)*

James Gadson *(Bill Withers, Freddie King, Martha Reeves, Marvin Gaye, Quincy Jones, Herbie Hancock, B.B. King, Albert King, Beck, et al.)*

Russell Kunkel *(Jackson Browne, James Taylor, Jimmy Buffett,*
Harry Chapin, J.J. Cale, Tracy Chapman, Crosby, Stills & Nash,
Neil Diamond, Bob Dylan, Dan Fogelberg, Arlo Guthrie,
Emmylou Harris, B.B. King, Carole King, Lyle Lovett,
Joni Mitchell, Linda Ronstadt, Carly Simon, Warren Zevon, et al.)

Gene Krupa *(Benny Goodman, et al.)*

Liberty DeVitto *(Billy Joel)*

Sidney "Big Sid" Catlett *(Benny Carter, Fletcher Henderson,*
Louis Armstrong, Benny Goodman, Dizzy Gillespie, et al.)

Art Blakey *(Thelonius Monk, Charlie Parker, Dizzy Gillespie,*
Horace Silver, Jazz Messengers, Lee Morgan, Freddie Hubbard,
Chick Corea, Keith Jarrett, et al.)

Joseph "Smokey" Johnson, Jr. *(Dave Bartholomew, Earl King,*
Professor Longhair, Fats Domino, Snooks Eaglin, et al.)

Odie Payne *(Muddy Waters, Jimmy Rogers, Otis Rush,*
Chuck Berry, Buddy Guy, et al.)

Carl Allen *(Freddie Hubbard, Jackie McLean, George Coleman,*
Phil Woods, et al.)

Tony Allen *(Fela Kuti)*

Buddy Rich *(Tommy Dorsey, Count Basie, Harry James,*
Charlie Parker, Dizzy Gillespie, Frank Sinatra, Ella Fitzgerald,
Louis Armstrong, et al.)

J.C. Heard *(Count Basie, Benny Carter, Louis Jordan,*
Louis Armstrong, Benny Goodman, Duke Ellington, et al.)

Clem Burke *(Blondie, The Romantics, The Ramones, Iggy Pop,*
Joan Jett, Eurhythmics, Pete Townshend, et al.)

Vernel Fournier *(Ahmad Jamal, Nancy Wilson, George Shearing,*
Clifford Jordan, et al.)

Keith Moon *(The Who)*

Gina Schock *(The Go-Go's)*

Bill Bruford *(Yes, King Crimson, Genesis, U.K., et al.)*

Neil Peart *(Rush)*

Vinnie Colaiuta *(Frank Zappa, Joni Mitchell, Herbie Hancock, Sting, Chick Corea, David Sanborn, Leonard Cohen, Ray Charles, Shawn Colvin, John Fogerty, Billy Joel, Al Jarreau, Jeff Beck, Paul McCartney, Glen Campbell, James Taylor, et al.)*

Warren "Baby" Dodds *(King Oliver's Creole Jazz Band, Louis Armstrong, et al.)*

Jeff Porcaro *(Toto, Steely Dan, Boz Scaggs, Michael Jackson, et al.)*

Chris Coleman *(Beck, Chaka Kahn, Rachelle Ferrell, et al.)*

Tony Williams *(Miles Davis, Eric Dolphy, Tony Williams Lifetime, Freddie Hubbard, et al.)*

Steve Jordan *(Stevie Wonder, Rolling Stones, John Mayer, Don Henley, John Mellencamp, Cat Stevens, Bob Dylan, Sonny Rollins, Cheryl Crow, Neil Young, James Taylor, et al.)*

Jim Gordon *(Delaney & Bonnie, Derek and the Dominos, Traffic, Frank Zappa, et al.)*

Kenny Aronoff *(John Mellencamp, Richard Thompson, Bob Seger, Melissa Etheridge, Smashing Pumpkins, Joe Cocker, et al.)*

Billy Cobham *(Miles Davis, Mahavishnu Orchestra, Horace Silver, Jack Bruce, Michael Brecker, Randy Brecker, et al.)*

Carter Beauford *(Dave Matthews band)*

Fred Below *(Chuck Berry, Bo Diddley, Jimmy Rogers, Howlin' Wolf, Otis Rush, Buddy Guy, Muddy Waters, et al.)*

Todd Sucherman *(Styx)*

Danny Seraphine *(Chicago)*

Tom Brechtlein *(Chick Corea, Robben Ford, Wayne Shorter, Al Di Meola, Jean-Luc Ponty)*

Kenwood Dennard *(George Clinton, Chick Corea, Dizzy Gillespie, Herbie Hancock, Jaco Pastorius, Whitney Houston, Sting, et al.)*

Mark Giuliana *(Meshell Ndegeocello, Dhafer Youseef, Wayne Krantz, Matisyahu, et al).*

Lewis Nash *(Betty Carter, Branford Marsalis, J.J. Johnson, Sonny Rollins, Stan Getz, Tommy Flanagan, et al.)*

Shawn Pelton *(Sheryl Crow, Shawn Colvin, Natalie Merchant, Elton John, Rod Stewart, Johnny Cash, et al.)*

Gavin Harrison *(King Crimson, Porcupine Tree, et al.)*

Dennis Chambers *(Parlament/Funkadelic, John Scofield, George Duke, Santana, Victor Wooten, Brecker Brothers, et al.)*

Daniel Glass *(Royal Crown Revue, Brian Setzer, Bette Middler, Liza Minelli, Marilyn Maye, Gene Simmons, et al.)*

Max Weinberg *(Bruce Springsteen & the E Street Band)*

Joe Saylor *(Stay Human, Roy Hargrove, Wynton Marsalis, Joe Lovano, et al.)*

Charles Connor *(Little Richard, Professor Longhair, James Brown, Smiley Lewis, Jack Dupree, et al.)*

Milt Turner *(Ray Charles, Hank Crawford, et al.)*

Connie Kay *(Modern Jazz Quartet, Milt Jackson, Lester Young, John Lewis, Paul Desmond, Miles Davis, Big Joe Turner, Ruth Brown, Sonny Rollins, Van Morrison, et al.)*

Clifton James *(Bo Diddley, Memphis Slim, Elmore James, et al.)*

Ed Blackwell *(Ornette Coleman, Don Cherry, Ray Charles, Ellis Marsalis, Old & New Dreams, et al.)*

Jeremy Steinkoler is a drummer, educator, and writer who lives in the San Francisco Bay Area with his wife and son. He is the Co-Founder and Co-Director of the award-winning BandWorks music program, is the Founder and Director of the East Bay Drum School and a Co-Founder of the Drummers Education Connection. He has performed multiple times at the Monterey and San Francisco Jazz Festivals and at the SXSW Music Festival. His music has earned numerous accolades and has been featured on the cover of *Jazz Inside* Magazine. Jeremy is proud to endorse Brooks Drums, Aquarian Drumheads, Sabian Cymbals, Vic Firth Drumsticks, Protection Racket Cases, Prologix Percussion, and Snareweight Drum Dampeners.

For more information, visit **jsteinkoler.com.**

Made in the USA
Middletown, DE
14 November 2023

42651576R00137